OKLAHOMA OUTLAW TALES

OKLAHOMA OUTLAW TALES

David A. Farris

LITTLE BRUCE
Edmond, Oklahoma

Oklahoma Outlaw Tales

Written by David A. Farris

Book Production, Michael S. Carter, Rocket Color

Second Edition
Copyright © 2004 by David A. Farris

First Edition
Copyright © 1999 by David A. Farris

Published by Little Bruce
P.O. Box 5991 • Edmond, Oklahoma 73083-5991

All rights reserved. No part of this work may be reproduced or transmitted in any form by any means without the written permission of the publisher.

Cover photo credit: *Archives & Manuscripts Division of the Oklahoma Historical Society.*

ISBN 0-9646922-3-6

Printed in the United States of America

For Aunt Alice.
(Alice Farris, 1915-2003)

Acknowledgments

The Oklahoma Historical Society

The Oklahombres

Dee Cordry

Herman Kirkwood

Rocket Color Printing

Ruby Wesson

Lois Rodriquez

The University of Oklahoma Library

OKOLHA
(Oklahoma • Outlaws • Lawmen • History • Association)

Oklahoma Territorial Museum

Table of Contents

Preface ....**xi**

Introduction ....**xiii**

Chapter One..**15**
Badmen From Robbers' Roost

Chapter Two..**25**
Ol' Yantis Becomes an Outlaw

Chapter Three...**31**
Battle on the Cimarron

Chapter Four **35**
Ned's Fort Mountain

Chapter Five..**49**
Hell-Fire at Ingalls

Chapter Six **59**
Cattle Annie and Little Britches

Chapter Seven **65**
A Badman Whose Word Was Good

Chapter Eight **75**
Christians From Hell

Chapter Nine **81**
The Reign of Terror in the Osage Hills

Chapter Ten **89**
Whiskey, Death and Good Times at Keokuk Falls

Chapter Eleven **101**
Four Men Hangin'

Chapter Twelve **123**
Dad's Story

Chapter Thirteen **129**
Elmer McCurdy's Excellent Adventure

Chapter Fourteen **137**
The End of the Trail

INDEX **141**

REFERENCES **143**

◆ Preface

The genre of the American Western has long been a setting for excitement and adventure. Books, movies and television certainly have done much to popularize this period of American history, beginning after the Civil War and ending just before the Roaring Twenties. As a child of the '70s, I grew up familiar with spaghetti westerns, John Wayne and the Cartrights, but wasn't necessarily a western fan.

It wasn't until the constraints and responsibilities of adulthood when I realized how much I enjoyed watching a good classic western. The Wild Bunch, Pat Garrett and Billy the Kid, and The Sons of Katie Elder became only a few of my favorite western movies. I made sure not to miss any of the documentaries concerning legends of the Old West that appeared on various cable stations and started a collection of books and articles on the subject. Despite my interest in the Old West, I wasn't sure exactly what it was that I found so appealing, then one day, it hit me; Westerns represent a freedom not found in modern day life. Of course, it also represented a freedom from law and order and a few other things people tend to take for granted. However, you still can find many people who would trade everything the modern world has to offer for an opportunity to have been born during the days of the Wild West.

I decided to write a fictional western taking place in Oklahoma. In order to familiarize myself with early Oklahoma, I spent time at the Oklahoma Historical Society and at my local public library. What I found was one fascinating story after another involving badmen, shoot-outs, Oklahoma landmarks and the lawmen charged with keeping order. These non-fiction tales of derring-do were more exciting than anything Hollywood had to offer.

As I collected these stories, I shared them with others, who like me, had not heard them before. It was amazing how few people seemed to be aware of these exciting events in Oklahoma history, including many Oklahomans. The plan became to take some of my favorite tales and compile them into concise accounts, complete with references. It was the same feeling I had that motivated me to write my first book, *Mysterious Oklahoma*. I was sure that if someone didn't compile these events for people to enjoy, they could be gone forever.

Many of the things we see in Hollywood westerns are as farfetched as the cowboy, dressed in white, who can ride the range all day without getting his clothes dirty. I wanted to capture the feeling of what it would have been like to live in Oklahoma Territory during such desperate days. There were frontier towns and communities who enjoyed most of life's modern conveniences just like they did "back East." However, you couldn't lose sight of the fact that you were in a potentially dangerous place that was certainly far from settled. Many badmen came to Indian Territory to hide from the law. A law-abiding citizen who wasn't willing to protect his property with a gun was just another potential victim.

Despite the dangers of life on the frontier, there existed a freedom, which to some, was an even swap. I can understand the feeling of civilization closing in around a person. I wish I had a wild place to ride free. The world is changing too fast; I only hope it's for the better. We still can relive those simpler, wild days of yesteryear in our minds as we muse over these non-fiction tales and wonder what it would have been like to be there.

Westerns continue to be popular because they represent the freedom of wide-open spaces and the challenge of new adventures. I wonder if people who lived during this period in history felt the same way? Even townspeople who enjoyed the most modern of conveniences were certainly roughing it by today's standards. The idea of living the rough and tumble life of an outlaw eventually would lose its romantic appeal to even the most adventuresome spirit. Most real-life outlaws lived desperate, miserable lives on the run from the law, until they died horrible, painful deaths. Still, we admire these reckless, free-spirits who had the grit and bravado to live by their own rules or die in defense of them.

David A. Farris

Introduction

Before Oklahoma became a state, it was a haven for outlaws. Law enforcement was sporadic and some towns went so far as to brag of having no law at all. To make things more conducive to those on the run, Oklahoma Territory, as it was known, was separated into land for settlers, Indian Territory, and No Man's Land, bringing jurisdiction into question.

In 1875, Judge Isaac Charles Parker, who presided over the federal bench in Fort Smith, Arkansas, was given jurisdiction over the neighboring Indian Territory to the west. His new charge was to become known as the territory "west of hell's fringe." The territories that bordered Oklahoma Territory were all becoming states. With statehood came investors; and no one wanted to risk his money where there was no law and order. To the outlaws not killed or jailed, Oklahoma Territory became a sanctuary. Judge Parker's U.S. Deputy Marshals would tangle with some of the most dangerous outlaws the Wild West had ever seen, desperate fugitives who had nowhere else to go and were determined to make a last stand rather than surrender.

Oklahoma Outlaw Tales is a compilation of colorful and exciting sagas from the land that would become the Sooner State. The tales in this book are non-fiction and are referenced. At some points, accounts of events were in conflict. When this became the case, Glenn Shirley's book, *West of Hell's Fringe* (University of Oklahoma Press, 1978), usually settled the dispute. I feel it is important to include all relative information to the stories, even if it means asking questions instead of answering them. I would rather leave events open-ended than imply I know everything about Oklahoma history.

The stories in this book are as diverse as the Oklahoma Territory it covers. From the rocky plateaus of the panhandle (Chapter One), to the sandy river basin of the Cimarron River (Chapter Three), to the wooded hills of Tahlequah (Chapter Four), the reader will experience a variety of stories. Some of these tales may differ from the way people have come to know them. It is my experience that sometimes misinformation can become history because people tell of events as they were told them, or as best they can remember. All I can do is list my sources and assure the reader of my goal to get the real story and demonstrate the hard, non-glamorous Sooner State.

Chapter 1

Badmen from Robbers' Roost

"Old Maid Rock near Black Mesa," the highest elevation in Oklahoma at 4,973 feet. *Photo Credit: Oklahoma Tourism Dept.*

In the heart of the American badlands lies 45 miles of lava rock-topped plateau spanning three states. In Colorado it's known as "Mesa de Maya." In New Mexico and Oklahoma it is known by its more popular English name, "Black Mesa."

Only three miles of Black Mesa reach into the northwest corner of the Oklahoma Panhandle. This area has always been popular with tourists dating as far back as the 1500s when Spanish explorers, including Coronado, crossed this region. By 1821, the historic Santa Fe Trail was blazed by Kit Carson. It became an important trade route linking the United States with Mexico until 1880, crossing through the Oklahoma Panhandle just a few miles south of Black Mesa. Tourists still come to this area of Oklahoma to visit Black Mesa Nature Preserve and Black Mesa State Park. On the nature preserve, in the same area with dinosaur remains and curious rock formations, can be found the highest point in Oklahoma reaching 4,973 feet above sea level (by the way, sea level is "0"). It is marked by a native

Badmen from Robbers' Roost   17

"Wedding Party Rocks near Black Mesa."
Photo Credit: Oklahoma Tourism Dept.

granite monument which may be viewed by visitors who are willing to hike up a 4.2 mile trail. Since the early 1800s, it was known as "Lookout Point" for obvious reasons; from here, one badman with a rifle could hold off a whole posse. Many outlaws have taken refuge in this notorious area, but none more infamous than the Bill Coe Gang.

Sometime in the early 1860s, during the Civil War, "Captain" Bill Coe, his brother and a few companions, came into the area of the Oklahoma Panhandle known as "No Man's Land." Until it became part of Oklahoma Territory by the Oklahoma Organic Act of 1890, No Man's Land was a place without law. There were a few sparse, dirty towns in this inhospitable stretch of short-grass land. These were places where vice ruled and order was maintained at the barrel of a gun. Captain Coe organized a band of cutthroats who robbed and terrorized travelers along the Santa Fe Trail, as well as homesteaders in the surrounding countryside. Around the year 1862, the Coe Gang found the rocky slopes of Lookout Point in the far southeast tip of the

Oklahoma Panhandle an ideal hideout. After selecting a site for their half-fort/half-residence, a barrier was erected and the walls were laid for a building which measured 35 feet by 16 feet and with a ceiling seven feet high. The gang used large rocks from the area to build a fortress that became the envy of any outlaw and was soon known to all as "Robbers' Roost."

The 30-inch thick walls of the hideout had no windows, but 27 portholes or "loopholes" as they were called, which came in handy for shooting at unwanted visitors. There were two doors at opposite ends of the one-room building; one on the north side and one to the south. At each end of the oblong structure stood chimneys for venting smoke from the two immense fireplaces providing both heat and light. One account even claimed the hideout was equipped with a piano and a full-sized bar.

By the foot of the mountain hideaway was a stream called the Carrizo, now known as North Carrizo Creek, which flowed into a junction connecting it with what was the Cimarron River, now known as the Dry Cimarron Scenic Byway. In the 1800s, the Cimarron River flowed freely, providing much needed water to farms and ranches built by homesteaders along the river's banks. This also meant there were prosperous neighbors to be robbed.

The numbers of the Coe Gang varied from 15 to 30 men on the average, but at its peak may have been as many as 50. Robbing travelers on the Santa Fe Trail was a good source of income for the gang but became too dangerous by 1865 when the troops from Fort Nichols, just 12 miles to the south in Colorado, were required to escort the wagon trains through the area. It became safer and more profitable to rustle cattle from homesteaders near and far. During the winter months, the horses and cattle were safely sheltered in the fertile lowlands around the Carrizo. When summer came, the livestock was trailed to faraway points in Colorado, Kansas, Texas and Wyoming to be sold.

The Coe Gang was more than a loose association of rogue badmen. The outlaws had a small farm near their headquarters they tended during the summer months to help meet the gang's basic needs. They were so well-organized as to have a bookkeeper to account for accumulated profits, as well as losses from unsold cattle.

In 1863, Juan Maria and Vincente Baca were perhaps the first permanent settlers in what was known as Cimarron County. They brought with them a large herd of sheep they had trailed from San Miguel County in New Mexico to an area in the Cimarron Valley about 10 miles away from Robbers' Roost. For some reason, the Coe Gang didn't bother their new neighbors, at least for the first three years. Perhaps this was because the sheep men were humble and struggling, but the best explanation may be that attacks on settlers would have caught the attention of the troops at Fort Nichols.

The heyday of the Coe Gang occurred toward the end of 1865. Fort Nichols was closed due to budget cuts. At this point, nothing was off limits and the gang had so many members it could split into two groups for simultaneous raids. Not only were homesteaders and travelers along the Santa Fe Trail in peril, but the gang became so brazen it repeatedly raided Fort Union in New Mexico, stealing government mules and horses.

In 1866, Juan Bernal and his brother Ramon trailed their flock of sheep from San Miguel County in New Mexico to the well-watered Cimarron Valley near Robbers' Roost. The Bernal Brothers were from Las Vegas, New Mexico, as was Vincente Baca. Perhaps it was word of Baca's prosperity that motivated the brothers to migrate, but they didn't count on the Coe Gang's reign of terror.

By 1867, the Bill Coe Gang all but assured its own demise by apparently thinking it was invincible. Members started off the year on the wrong foot in February when they attacked the Bernal homestead, killing three of their men and driving off two flocks of sheep. Each flock counted 1700 head, a loss the Bernal Brothers could not endure. Ramon Bernal followed the outlaws as they drove the sheep in the direction of Pueblo, Colorado, which at that time was just a small frontier post. Incredibly, the Coe Gang apparently underestimated the tenacity of the Bernal Brothers who, probably with the help of their neighbors—Baca, Maria and everyone's combined employees—managed to recover their sheep and return them to the Cimarron Valley.

Undaunted by this defeat, the Coe Gang carried out a raid on Fort Lyon in Colorado, stealing horses and mules as they did at Fort Union. Troops from Fort Lyon tracked the outlaws back to the Carrizo at the foot of Robbers' Roost as other stock owners had been doing for years. The problem was breaking the wall of secrecy protecting the outlaws and their activities. This was solved when a spy from Fort Lyon was able to infiltrate the gang and learn the details of their numerous depravations.

The troops from Fort Lyon retaliated early one morning when they surprised 11 of Coe's men who were sleeping in an abandoned shack. According to a rumor, the outlaws were all hanged on the spot. Captain Coe was captured a short while later, but was able to escape.

Historians agree the Coe Gang's reign of terror was ended early one morning in late 1867 by a cannon retrieved from Fort Lyon more than 100 miles away. It is also agreed there was an unsuccessful attack on Robbers' Roost before the cannon was retrieved. What is in question is who attacked Robbers' Roost before the cannon was ordered. One account gives credit to a "Mr. Allen," Sheriff of Bent County, Colorado, for leading a posse intent on capturing the outlaw gang. The other version is that it was a contingent of 25 regulars from "the fort on the Arkansas River" commanded by General W.H. Penrose. Regardless of who mounted the first attack, the sight of an unsuccessful group of attackers withdrawing in defeat must have done much to boost the egos of the already swell-headed Coe Gang.

The men from the first attack returned with troops and a cannon from Fort Lyon but kept out of sight from the outlaws. Under the cover of night, the artillery field piece was dragged up the mesa and set up on a bluff on the north side of Carizzo Creek, just overlooking the outlaws' fortress.

In the morning, the Coe Gang finally caught a glimpse of the cannon. They were awed, but apparently underestimated its destructive force. Since the gang knew surrender would mean certain death at the end of a rope, it made sense to hole up in their outlaw fortress which had served so well in the past. Of course, hindsight dictates they should have made a break for it when they had the chance.

The attack by cannon was brief, but served its purpose as the outlaws retaliated with an ineffective volley of rifle shots. Although over a mile from his target, the gunner's aim was good enough to send a cannon ball six inches in diameter, shattering one corner of the fortress. With the fortress in ruins and the troops quickly advancing, it was every outlaw for himself. Those not dead or wounded had a choice to make: either a desperate last stand or make a run for it; either way they lost. Those who ran later were rounded up and hanged, and those who stood were shot to pieces by the militia who were excellent marksmen.

In the confusion of his gang's shooting it out and being killed, Captain Coe bravely secured his horse and fled towards the upper Cimarron.

Coe utilized a strategy of riding and hiding to remain one step ahead of his pursuers who were hot on his trail. He made it to the ranch of the Emery Family who had recently taken residence along the banks of the Cimarron River about 20 miles north of the town of Folsom, New Mexico. Coe was allowed to take refuge, but with a posse close behind, his stay was brief. In 1868, after reaching the mesa north of the Cimarron at Folsom, Captain Bill Coe was finally captured when he surrendered to troops who had him hopelessly surrounded.

Bill Coe was taken to Pueblo, Colorado. He wasn't hanged on the spot like his men, because of the large reward for his capture; under such circumstances it was better to produce a live prisoner to verify your claim. Unfortunately, for the outlaw, the local citizens had no patience for the court. Captain Coe and his gang were feared and hated to a point that frontier justice would prevail. He was taken from jail by a lynch mob and hanged from a cottonwood tree near Fountain Creek while awaiting trial. An almost predictable end for a badman of such notariety.

The ruins of many old outlaw hideouts are associated with tales of lost treasure, and Robbers' Roost is no exception. Black Mesa has changed little since the days of Captain Coe. Rumors of the Coe Gang's lost treasure haunt this rocky region.

In 1920, Elzy Tanner purchased 160 acres of land, which includ-

An Indian corn grinding site at Black Mesa, in Oklahoma.
Photo Credit: Archives & Manuscripts Division of the Oklahoma Historical Society.

ed Robbers' Roost and the surrounding area. He soon learned just how strong was the lure of these old treasure tales. Almost immediately, he had to run off tresspassers, sometimes at the barrel of a gun.

No treasure has been found. The only things of real value on the land are acres of petrified wood and many varieties of decorative rock used for landscaping.

As the years go by, the remains of Robbers' Roost continue to erode but are still visible. The remains are currently on private property, and may be visited with proper permission. Anyone interested in seeing the old outlaw fortress may contact the Boise City Chamber of Commerce.

Oklahoma is awash in stories of ill-fated badmen and their unclaimed plunder. Outlaws from all over North America rode into Oklahoma Territory with the law hot on their trail. One can only wonder how many luckless outlaws had been killed by lawmen or died in prison before they had the opportunity to retrieve their well-hidden loot.

Legends from Robbers' Roost suggest that the area around any unusual landmark may be a good place for modern day treasure hunters to explore; with the land owner's permission, of course. These stories remind us of how little history is actually known, and how much is still out there, waiting to be discovered.

Chapter 2
Ol' Yantis Becomes An Outlaw

Oliver (Ol') Yantis (sometimes misspelled Yountis) was the first new member of the Doolin Gang. The Doolin Gang was what became of the Dalton Gang after their ill-fated attempt to rob two banks at once in Coffeyville, Kansas. Bill Doolin probably would have been among the dead had he not had trouble with his horse. As it was, Bob Dalton, Emmett Dalton, Grat Dalton, Bill Powers and Dick Broadwell were shot to pieces by the good folks of Coffeyville. Emmett Dalton, who was the only survivor despite his many wounds, was sent to prison. Bill Doolin replaced Bob Dalton as the gang's new leader and with Charley Pierce and George "Bitter Creek" Newcomb became the nucleus of what would become the Bill Doolin Gang.

Yantis farmed cotton on a homestead occupied by his sister Mrs. Hugh McGinn, three miles southeast of Orlando in northeastern Logan County. It was near here, along Beaver Creek in May of 1891, where the Dalton Gang had stolen a herd of fine horses from a colony of settlers from Missouri. Yantis and his sister aided and abetted the gang by bringing them food and keeping an eye out for the law.

The disastrous robbery at Coffeyville should have been a lesson to any would-be outlaw, but Doolin didn't seem to have any trouble recruiting new members for his gang. In the case of Yantis, life as an outlaw must have appeared more exciting than that of a cotton farmer. On the night of October 13, 1892, a stocky, dark-complexioned man with a mustache fitting Yantis' description was reported as one of the members of the new Doolin Gang who robbed a train from Wharton, a small weigh station 30 miles north of Guthrie. The gang used the heavy patches of timber in the vicinity of the McGinn claim to hide out after the robbery.

On November 1, 1892, in the company of Doolin and Newcomb, Yantis took part in his last robbery. The masked trio rode slowly into the town of Spearville, Kansas on a cold, cloudy day when few people were on the streets. The men stopped in front of the Ford County Bank, where Yantis watched the horses while Doolin and Newcomb stepped inside with their Winchesters to make a withdrawal.

If the gang would have taken a few more minutes to check the vault, they would have noticed $1,697 in First National Bank of Dodge City and U.S. Treasury notes. However, they grabbed only the cash on hand. In just three minutes the gang was back on their horses with the money. No one had noticed the robbers, until they fired several shots in the air before riding out of town to the south. As the gang made their getaway, they caught the attention of a group of hunters returning home. The two groups exchanged about 15 shots, but no one was hit. A few of the townspeople mounted their horses and attempted to follow the trio, but the outlaws' thoroughbreds left them in the dust. With Yantis following the veteran outlaws, the Doolin Gang disappeared into the Arkansas hills. Sheriff Chalkley M.(Chalk) Beeson rallied a posse to chase down the bank robbers, but turned back after the trail crossed over into Oklahoma. Despite first impressions, Sheriff Beeson hadn't quit the chase. He just had a better idea to find the money.

At last, the trio of bank robbers crossed into the safety of Indian Territory. At a place known as the Outlet, the gang relaxed and divided their money. After making plans to meet later at their Cimarron hideout, the gang split up to confuse any die-hard trackers. Yantis headed home to his sister's farm.

Back in Dodge City, Sheriff Beeson mailed penny postcards to towns and weigh stations in the area where the outlaws might be heading. He described the three bank robbers, the large-numbered new five dollar bills issued by the First National Bank of Dodge City, Kansas, and the $450 reward offered by the bank. It wasn't long before Hamilton B. (Ham) Hueston, brother of Stillwater's Marshal Tom Hueston, responded to Sheriff Beeson's query. Yantis was known in the town of Stillwater where his mother kept the Commercial Hotel. Hueston recognized the description of Yantis and his dun pony with a dark mane and tail. Sheriff Beeson sent a man who had seen the three bank robbers to Stillwater to see if he recognized the suspect. On November 25, Hueston and the witness rode from Stillwater 20 miles west to the McGinn place. Under the pretext of looking for horses to buy, the men asked Yantis if any of his neighbors had any for sale. As the duo rode away, the witness identified the obviously nervous man as one of the robbers.

On the night of November 29, Sheriff Beeson, Marshal Tom Hueston, Ham Hueston and a constable named George Cox began their ride to Orlando to make an arrest. The posse reached the McGinn place the following morning, just before dawn. They positioned themselves between the house and the barn, hoping to surprise the outlaw when he came to feed his horse. About a half hour later at daybreak, a man holding a feed bag peered from the house through the morning fog to see if the coast was clear. As he cautiously made his way to the barn, Ham Hueston whispered to Beeson, "That is Ol' Yantis." From a distance of about 50 feet, Sheriff Beeson stood up and called for the outlaw to surrender. Yantis answered by dropping his feed sack, drawing a revolver from his shoulder holster and firing a wild shot in the direction of the lawman's voice. Ham aimed his new shotgun at the outlaw, but when he pulled the trigger it misfired. Yantis fired in the direction of the shotgun's "click" sound, but again missed his target. At this point, Marshal Hueston, Sheriff Beeson and Constable Cox fired at the outlaw at once, causing their shots to sound like just one. Yantis toppled back, mortally wounded but still full of fight. As he fell to the ground, Yantis fired the remaining rounds in his gun, then reloaded. The other lawmen were ready to finish him, but Sheriff Beeson intervened by shouting, "Don't shoot again, he's done for."

Due to the distance, fog and dim morning light, there was concern the outlaw could get away. As the lawmen closed in, a bullet grazed Cox, who then swore he'd finish the outlaw. Beeson again interfered saying, "He's too badly injured to escape." Suddenly Mrs. McGinn came running from the house into the yard screaming, "Run, Ol', run! For God's sake, don't kill him!" Sheriff Beeson called out to her that there was one way she could save his life; persuade him to surrender. Reluctantly, Mrs. McGinn went to her brother, picked up his gun and handed it to Beeson. The posse moved in to arrest the dying outlaw. Yantis was spared one serious wound when a lawmen's bullet had struck his heavy leather pocketbook containing money from the

Ol' Yantis Becomes An Outlaw 29

Oliver Yantis, alias Cresent Sam, in a casket.
Photo Credit: **Western History Collections, University of Oklahoma Libraries.**

Spearville robbery. This resulted in a bloody mess of torn bills, instead of a fatality.

However, another round struck his right side at a downward angle, severing his spine. Yantis was bleeding to death. The posse patched his wounds as best they could and loaded the outlaw on a wagon to take him to Orlando and the nearest doctor. Despite everyone's best efforts, Oliver "Ol" Yantis died a few hours later at one o'clock p.m. Three days later, the local paper in Edmond, Oklahoma reported that the outlaw was not expected to live.

Fifty-five dollars in blood-stained, bullet-torn currency from the robbery was proof the posse had one of the right men. Sheriff Beeson was paid the $450 reward from the bank of which he gave the other posse members $50 each.

In the spring of 1893, Marshal Hueston was sued for $20,000 by S.J. Yantis for the killing of her husband. Prior to the lawsuit, territorial officials had no knowledge of Ol' Yantis ever having been married. The case was dismissed, re-filed, and dismissed by a higher court on the grounds that the posse had acted under legal warrant and authority.

Ol' Yantis was game to the end. Even after being mortally wounded, he admitted to nothing, told no names and never asked for mercy. He was a young man fully aware of the potential consequences of his new career. When the game turned against him, he still played out his hand and took his medicine. It wasn't long after that the rest of the Doolin Gang would learn how brave they would be when faced with their own mortality.

Chapter 3
Battle on the Cimarron

On April 4, 1895, along the Cimarron River near the town of Ames in Major County, one desperate, hell-firin' gun battle occurred between lawmen and members of the Doolin Gang. The editor of the *Hennessey Clipper* referred to the shoot-out as a fight "without parallel in the annals of Oklahoma." When the battle ended 45 minutes later, there was one man dead and more than 200 rounds fired.

The gunfight was the result of one-half of a posse's catching up with the Doolin Gang who had robbed the Rock Island train at Dover, Oklahoma, the night before. Tulsa Jack, Bitter Creek Newcomb, Charley Pierce, Bill Raidler and Red Buck Waightman were once again putting distance between them and lawmen charged with bringing them to justice. Within hours, U.S. Deputy Marshal Chris Madsen was notified of the robbery. By 3:00 a.m., Madsen and 11 other deputy marshals headed north from El Reno in a special box car provided by the railroad. At daybreak, the posse picked up the easy-to-follow tracks the outlaws made no effort to hide. It was later learned that the outlaws had intended to bushwhack the posse, but they probably didn't plan on the marshal's quick response. The posse followed the outlaws to the sandy hills and basins around the Cimarron River. Madsen decided the group should split up in order to cover more ground more quickly. He took five men and circled to the south and west, leaving Deputy Banks, Captain Prather, J.H. Clary, John Phelps, M.S. Hutchison and W.E. (Billie) Moore to head the other direction.

Around two o'clock that afternoon, Banks and his men topped a sand basin to see a man standing guard by some horses and four men asleep in a grove of blackjack trees. At the same time, the guard saw the posse and alerted the sleeping gang. Billie Moore yelled at the outlaws, "Throw up your hands, you sons-of-bitches." The outlaws didn't feel compelled to comply and responded to the lawman's request with rifle fire. Because one of the lawmen had to watch the horses, the sides were evenly matched, five against five. The outlaws, however, had the advantage of each having a Winchester chambered for the .45/90 cartridge. Despite firing from lighter weapons, the lawmen bravely stood their ground as the outlaws' rifles kicked up sand all around them. Towards the end of the 45 minute battle, the posse seemed to be gaining the advantage, forcing the outlaws to make a run for it. The outlaws retreated to a hollow not covered by the posse and mounted their horses, firing their guns as they fled. The posse converged on the outlaws' campsite to find one dead man, one dead horse and the blood of wounded gang members. No one in the posse recognized the dead outlaw. With the help of a local farmer, Prather and Banks brought the body to Hennessey, while the rest of the posse followed the outlaws' trail from their campsite. The outlaws got away, but a few miles down the trail the posse came upon another dead horse, its saddle covered with outlaw blood. One year later, a Guthrie newspaper reported the horse in question belonged to Bill Raidler who had his finger shattered by a bullet from the posse. It was hanging by skin and muscle, so the outlaw simply took out his pocket knife, severed the useless digit and threw it away.

 The posse continued to follow the outlaws' trail. At sundown, they reached the farm of an old preacher named Godfry, whom the gang had killed while stealing his horses. The lawmen followed the gang's trail west through the night. By now, the outlaws had been joined by two more members of the gang. The next morning the posse rode into the town of Vilas, where the outlaws once again had changed horses just two hours earlier. The terrain had changed, making tracking more difficult. Marshal Madsen and his men returned to El Reno later that day after losing the outlaws' trail in the foothills of the Glass Mountains. The Doolin Gang once again had gotten away with the loot, however any adulation would be short-lived. The boys didn't know it yet, but the Dover train robbery marked the end of the Doolin Gang.

 Back in Hennessey, officials were attempting to determine the identity of the outlaw killed during the Cimarron River shoot-out. Hundreds of people viewed the body, but no one in town recognized the man. Deputies Banks and Prather took the corpse to El Reno, where it was viewed by hundreds more citizens who couldn't identify the man. In frustration, the mystery man was moved to Oklahoma City where he was displayed, in his coffin, in the hall of the court house. After hundreds more citizens gawked at the morbid spectacle, a man named H.R. Whirtzell from Sterling, Kansas was finally able to identify the departed outlaw as a man who once worked for him named William Blake, better known as Tulsa Jack. With the body identified, rewards totaling $3,000 would be divided equally among the six deputies involved in the Cimarron River shoot-out. The body of Tulsa Jack Blake was returned to El Reno where it was finally laid to rest.

After losing the posse in the foothills of the Glass Mountains, the gang paused for a moment to plan their next move. The outlaws decided to go their separate ways in order to frustrate any lawmen who might try to pick up their trail. The robbers had no way of knowing, but that was the last time they would be united as members of the Doolin Gang. The outcome might have been different if the gang had robbed the Dover train a few years earlier. By 1895, Judge Parker's U.S. Deputy Marshals had become more organized and efficient. Within a year of the Dover train robbery, four of the five participants would be killed by lawmen and one would be sentenced to a lengthy term in prison.

Bill Raidler was wounded while resisting arrest by U.S. Deputy Marshal Bill Tilghman, who made the arrest, anyway. Raidler was paroled in 1903, due to developing locomotor ataxia as a result of his wounds. He was too ill to return to outlawry and died a few years later.

Times had changed in Indian Territory. Homesteaders were settling in the area, towns were being established and wild ideas like "statehood" were being discussed. All of these events were contingent upon the establishment of law and order. Before long, lawmen would have the challenge of chasing outlaws who drove V-8 powered cars and toted those new-fangled machine guns. It's important to remember the Doolin Gang was emulating the James and Dalton Gangs whose glory days long since had passed. Like it or not, Indian Territory was approaching the twentieth century.

Chapter 4
Ned's Fort Mountain

Ned Christie was the last great Cherokee warrior who managed to elude Judge Parker's top lawmen longer than any other outlaw in Indian Territory. Most outlaws survived by hiding and living life on the run, however, Christie had a different strategy. He made a stand where he lived in the hills near Tahlequah and challenged the law to come and get him. For six years, Christie ran free and enjoyed a well-deserved reputation as a crack-shot, deadly with his firearms.

Ned Christie was born in Rabbit Trap, Indian Territory in 1852. He was a full-blooded Cherokee Indian from a well-respected family who provided him with a stable upbringing enjoyed by few outlaws. Ned's father, Watt Christie, was a gunsmith who taught his trade to his son. The elder Christie was a respected and well-liked tribal member who wanted his son to follow in his footsteps. Ned was intelligent, spoke English well and was recognized for his leadership abilities. In time he became a cultured member of the Cherokee Council and was elected to the Cherokee Legislature. Eventually he served in both houses of the Council and served in the Keytoyah Society.

As a respected council member who served with honor and distinction, it seemed the Christie family values had paid off in regards to Ned. He was a popular gunsmith and blacksmith around the Tahlequah area. His talent as a gunsmith was evident in a famous photo of the man and his guns. It showed Christie holding his rifle of choice, a Winchester Model 1873, by the barrel with his left hand and presenting one of a pair of unusual revolvers with his right (the other revolver was tucked into a holster on his gun belt, worn in a cross-draw fashion). The pair of pistols was originally Colt 1860 Army percussion revolvers in .44 caliber. Percussion revolvers, unlike cartridge-firing revolvers, are less convenient to load because each chamber of the cylinder must first be loaded with a charge of powder, then a lead ball is mashed down from the front. Finally, a powder charge is placed on the opposite end. This time-consuming routine must be repeated at least four more times to load the pistol (Although there were six chambers in the cylinder, it was best to load only five so the hammer rested safely on an empty chamber. This is still an important practice today if a revolver is not equipped with a hammer-block style of safety!). However, some shooters preferred the 1860 style because of its balance, which enhanced the shooter's ability to quickly draw, fire and hit one's target. Christie enjoyed the best of both worlds by converting the pair of Colts to fire the same .44/40 cartridges for which his rifle was chambered. The photo shows that the seating lever (used for packing the powder charge and lead ball into the chambers of the cylinder) was removed and an ejector rod housing was attached in order to remove the spent cartridge shells from the cylinder's chambers. Christie then had to cut a notch in the back end of the guns for loading, which would be a simple task when compared to the fitting of the cylinders. According to modern day firearm experts, the cylinder of the Colt 1860 Army revolver would not have been long enough for the .44/40 cartridge. This would imply Christie had to create and drill his own cylinders. Not only was he a skilled machinist, but to lay out the chamber holes would have required a working knowledge of trigonometry.

It wasn't long before Christie settled in a remote cabin with his wife and their son. Life was good for the talented, intelligent leader of his Cherokee people, but fate was right around the corner.

Ned Christie was a man to be admired. However, like most men, he did have faults. He patronized the bootleggers who traveled through Indian Territory selling liquor (often referred to as "who hit John") despite prohibition. Although it was illegal to buy, sell or even possess alcoholic beverages in the area, lawmen usually didn't consider the enforcement of such laws a priority. This played a role in the death of U.S. Deputy Marshal Dan Maples, although accounts of the events surrounding the shooting would differ.

Almost every book or article about Ned Christie has stated that he killed Marshal Maples; case closed. This is because many of the earlier books about outlaws were written by former lawmen and their accounting of such events were thought to be indisputable. As with most things in life, there were at least two sides to every story and the events described by lawmen were usually told in their favor.

Early accounts of how Christie killed Marshal Maples were recounted in later writings and along with other myths told as fact.

The most accurate and thoroughly researched publication dealing with Ned Christie and the death of Marshal Maples is *The Killing of Ned Christie* (Reliance Press, 1990) by Bonnie Speer. She refers to an article from the June 9, 1918, Sunday edition of the *Daily Oklahoman*, entitled, "Cherokee Indian, Killed For A Murder He Didn't Commit, Exonerated After 30 Years." According to Mrs. Speer and the *Daily Oklahoman*, Marshal Maples was killed by an Indian named Bud Trainor.

Ned Christie was in the town of Tahlequah, Oklahoma for a special session of the National Council to decide what action should be taken in regard to the burning of a female seminary. On the night of May 4, 1887, Christie, unarmed, had left the home where he was staying to buy some whiskey. He walked downtown where he ran into a half-blood friend of his named John Parris who knew where they could buy some liquor. The men crossed over the Spring Branch Creek on a footlog bridge, headed for "Dog Town" and the cabin of Nancy Shell. She invited the men inside, where they were greeted by Bud Trainor who was eating supper. Christie and Parris each bought a bottle of whiskey from the bootlegger. She tore a strip of cloth from her apron to make a stopper for one of the bottles, then handed it to Christie who put it in the pocket of his black coat.

Christie and Parris left Shell's cabin after the sun had set and the night was growing dark. Close by, at the edge of the woods, the pair met John Hogshooter, George Parris and Charley Bobtail. The men talked and laughed between sips of whiskey and soon became intoxicated as they wandered towards upper Spring Branch Creek. Around 8:00 p.m., Christie said he was going back to his boardinghouse and stumbled down the path to the footlog bridge. However, he never crossed the creek, instead collapsing into some bushes and passing out for the night.

In the town of Tahlequah, word that Marshal Maples was in town and had plans to arrest a couple of the local bootleggers was making the rounds. Bud Trainor was friendly with people in the illegal liquor business and took it upon himself to take care of the marshal. He was seen by many people on his way to the footlog bridge with a large revolver stuck in his pants. Trainor crossed over to the other side of the creek to find Christie passed out in the bushes. He removed the sleeping man's black coat and put it on over his white shirt. The would-be bushwacker took a position behind a bending tree to wait for the marshal to return to where he and his men were camped. At this point in the story we learn there was a witness to the shooting. However, Trainor was so feared, no one dared to tell the real story. Even after his death in 1896, those who knew the truth feared retribution from members of his gang.

Richard A. "Dick" Humphrey was a 56-year-old blacksmith who was on his way to Dog Town to get a drink after a long day of work. He was an ex-slave who, with his parents, was adopted into the Cherokee Nation after the Civil War. As he approached the footlog bridge, he had witnessed Trainor preparing for the ambush. Humphrey was afraid to let Trainor know he was there, so he stood still and watched. It wasn't long before Marshal Maples, accompanied by George Jefferson, approached the bridge from the other side of the creek. Jefferson was in front and saw the muzzle of the gun against the tree. "Don't shoot," he called out, but Trainor didn't listen. He fired a round at Marshal Maples, sending a bullet into his right breast and exiting below his shoulder blade. Mortally wounded, the lawman fell, but recovered enough to draw his pistol and fire, nicking the whiskey bottle with the apron stopper in the pocket of Christie's coat. All three men quickly fired their revolvers until empty, with no one else getting hit. Jefferson shouted to Peel who was in the camp, but close enough to hear, to come running with a gun. Trainor ran to Christie, threw him his coat, then shook him in an attempt to get him to run. Christie staggered a short distance, then lay down near a clump of trees where Trainor left him. Marshal Maples was taken back downtown to the nearest doctor, but despite all efforts, he bled to death shortly after midnight. The lawmen soon learned about the five Indians who were drinking by the footlog bridge and immediately considered them suspects. Ned Christie slept, unaware of the developing events that would change his life.

Christie awoke the next morning and headed back to town. On the way, he encountered a friend who informed him of the previous night's events and that he was accused of killing the marshal. Christie was scared and confused. He didn't trust the white man's court to give him a fair trial. He consulted his father for advice, knowing the news would break the old man's heart.

"Give yourself up, son," Watt Christie pleaded. "Face the charges. It's the only way." Rather than face the music, Ned made the decision to take the "owl hoot trail" until he could prove his innocence. The news of the death of Dan Maples angered and outraged the citizens in his hometown of Bentonville, Arkansas. Three of Judge Parker's top U.S. Deputy Marshals were assigned to investigate the case. Ned Christie was soon charged as the shooter and his name was added to a long list of Indian Territory outlaws. The marshals expected they eventually would get their man, but had no idea how great a challenge this would become. Ned Christie was well-liked by his friends and neighbors in Indian Territory and was viewed as a victim of circumstance who was hounded by angry, white lawmen. For the next six years, Christie wielded a reign of terror so vicious as to change the minds of his most devout partisans.

Christie could have collected his family and left the territory, but instead decided to hole up with them in their remote cabin near Tahlequah. Lawmen learned of its location but had no success in making an arrest. During the summer of 1887, there were at least two attempts by U.S. Marshals to serve justice; the first resulted in Deputy Joe Bowers' being shot in the leg, the latter with Deputy John Fields' being wounded by a bullet to the neck. A few months later in early 1888, a federal posse tried its hand at taking the cabin. This time Christie showed mercy and wounded only three deputies. Not only were the lawmen waging war against a crack shot with a clear view of all surrounding terrain, but it was nearly impossible for a posse of white men to sneak up on an Indian in Indian Territory. Christie's friends and neighbors alerted him about the approaching posses then stayed around to help out in the fight. Christie and his friends had plenty of time to ready themselves for battle before the lawmen would be within range of their rifles.

Christie ran free through the Tahlequah area for the next year despite the best efforts of Judge Parker's marshals. By 1889, U. S. Deputy Marshal Heck Thomas had devised a strategy to get the drop on Christie. The marshal led a posse the long way around into Indian Territory avoiding the watchful eyes of Christie's neighbors. The plan worked, until the posse got close enough to the cabin to alert Christie's dogs. When the barking began, so did the gunfire. During the battle, posse members were able to set fire to his workshop. The fire soon spread to the main cabin causing the Christie family to make a break for it. As Christie's wife and son fled, the posse cowardly opened fire on them. Both were able to make their escape into the woods, even though the boy had been seriously wounded, shot in the hip and lung. Ned Christie remained in his burning home and fired angrily at the posse to cover his family's escape. He drew a bead on U.S. Deputy Marshal L. P. Isabel and sent a round smashing through his shoulder, crippling his arm for life. During the battle, Marshal Thomas fired a 400 grain slug from his .45/70 caliber Winchester Model 1886 rifle into Christie's face. Despite having the bridge of his nose shattered and his left eye put out, Christie survived. He was rescued by his neighbors as flames consumed the cabin.

The Christie family made it to an Indian doctor who patched their wounds. The story of the raid on the Christie cabin invoked sympathy from the residence of Indian Territory. The marshals knew bringing Ned Christie to justice would be no easy task, but now he was perceived as a martyr of blood-thirsty lawmen.

It seems Christie believed he was an innocent victim of circumstance because of his next action. Here again was a perfect opportunity to flee the territory with his family into the safety of obscurity. Instead, he decided to make a stand to spite Judge Parker, his marshals and his law. Christie was seething with anger and hatred. At this point, he made a vow never to speak a word of the white man's English and would communicate only in his native Cherokee language. The next four years, he waged a reign of terror, including robbery, arson and more death. With the help of his neighbors, Christie made plans for a structure of such magnitude that over 100 years later the hilltop location still would be referred to as "Ned's Fort Mountain." The battles that occurred at this site became the stuff of legend surpassing even the most contrived Hollywood fiction.

Ned Christie knew the old ways of his Cherokee people. When they were a warring tribe, they lived in walled forts for protection. Christie selected a hilltop location by Rabbit Trap Canyon, about a half mile from his burned-down cabin. With the help of family and neighbors, a two-story fortress with walls two logs thick was built. The outside walls of the fortress were fortified with rock and the inside was lined with two-by-fours for added security. The surrounding trees and bushes were cleared away to prevent any sneak attacks and a lookout platform was constructed giving the appointed sentry a view of the entire valley along Bitting Creek, which flowed at the foot of the hill. The fort was well-stocked with food, water and ammunition. It was here Christie would make his stand and dare all attackers. Although the area of the fort was remote, it was not by any means hidden. It was not the outlaw's intention to lay low. When the structure was complete, Christie sent word to Marshal Thomas of his whereabouts and extended an invitation to come by and shoot it out; Thomas declined. U.S. Deputy Marshal Dave Rusk was one of the first lawmen to challenge Christie's stronghold. Rusk lived in the nearby town of Oaks where he operated a store with the help of his family. In 1891, Marshal Rusk with a posse of Indians mounted one of the first recorded attacks of Ned's Fort Mountain. At the time of the attack, Christie was being visited by neighbors who helped drive away the posse with apparently little effort. After several members of the posse were wounded, the men retreated. Despite the Marshal's defeat, he had the tenacity to mount at least two more attempts to bring in the outlaw. On each occasion, the lawman never even got a chance to talk to Christie before being driven away by rifle fire.

Another attempt to roust Christie from his sanctuary occurred on October 11, 1892. The report described how the unnamed lawmen devised a plan to burn down the fort. A wagon loaded with brush was set afire and pushed down a hill towards the cabin. Unfortunately for the lawmen, the only structure burned to the ground that night was an outhouse the wagon collided with when it veered off course. The lawmen went to plan "B," which was to throw lighted sticks of dynamite at the outlaws. This strategy had less effect than the burning of the outhouse. At least the loss of the outhouse caused the outlaws some inconvenience, as opposed to the dynamite, which simply bounced off the fort and exploded, having no effect. After awhile, the demoralized lawmen called it a day and went home.

Ned Christie had one of the longest and most dynamic criminal careers of any outlaw in Judge Isaac Parker's jurisdiction. His skills as a gunman and the support of his Cherokee neighbors did much to help him in his efforts. In addition, there are those who would suggest he was also aided by forces beyond those of mortal man. As the story goes, Christie had a brother-in-law named Seed Wilson who lived near Locust Grove in Indian Territory and was a full-blood Cherokee medicine man. When Christie first went "on the scout," he sent for Seed to visit him in his cabin. The medicine man spent three weeks going through ancient Cherokee ceremonies in order to put a "spell" on Christie. When Seed returned home, he admitted to a neighbor he had visited Christie. When asked if the badman were safe, he responded, "Yes, marshals no catch him now." Whether it was skill or spirits, for many years after, Christie was unbeatable in battle.

The full extent of Christie's crimes may never be known. He was seething with anger and channeled it into challenging Judge Parker's authority. Christie collected a group of full-blood Indian friends he led on robbing raids on isolated settlements. In their wake, Christie was credited with a death toll of eight men, one woman and a half-blooded boy. Towards the end of his career, his crimes became so extreme that even the Cherokee leaders urged their tribe to turn against their brother; and perhaps, so did the ancient Cherokee spirits who protected him. In any event, Ned Christie's luck was about to change.

Despite the forces protecting him, Christie had summoned many forces to the contrary. Judge Parker and his marshals had endured the outlaw for too long. The lawmen realized the magnitude of their objective and knew they were in for a battle. U.S. Marshal Jacob Yoes ordered his deputy Paden Tolbert to assemble a posse to once again challenge Christie and his gang. Before the attack, Paden and three men rode to Coffeyville, Kansas to retrieve a three-pound cannon. When they returned, the four lawmen rendezvoused with the rest of the posse in the Cookson Hills on the night of November 1, 1892. The following morning, before dawn, the men made their way through the oak and pine trees in the early morning mist to wage a war they were determined to win.

The fort was inhabited by Christie and two other outlaws: Charlie Hare, a young Cherokee who recently had joined the gang, and Arch Wolfe, another young cattle thief who was wanted by the law. Wolfe was on guard duty while his partners slept. From his lookout, he saw one of the lawmen creep across a small clearing to the safety of a tree. Wolfe began firing at the figure and the fight was on. Christie, who slept with his Winchester in his hands, sprang to life, as did Hare, and sent the posse running for cover from the volley of rifle fire. The lawmen took cover and returned fire, even though they must have been aware by now it was a futile effort. The exchange of rifle fire continued for hours before the cannon was positioned in range of the fort. Placing the cannon in a strategic location would be a dangerous task. In desperation, the lawmen placed boards on the cannon to shield them from the outlaws' constant and well-placed rifle fire. When the cannon fire began, the posse was amazed at the sight of three-pound projectiles bouncing off the fort doing little or no damage. Regardless, the cannon was fired at the fort 30 times until the breech of the weapon split. Despite their best-laid plans, the posse was no closer to arresting Christie than they were six years ago. After all this time and effort, the thought of Christie's once again getting the better of the lawmen in battle was too bitter a pill to swallow. The exchange of rifle fire continued into the night. Under the cover of darkness, deputies Bill Smith and Charlie Copeland, broke their cover to build a rolling barricade of their own. Wood and rocks were piled on the remains of a burned lumber wagon used during a previous assault (probably the same one that burned down the outhouse), then it was rolled within about 22 yards from the fort. Tolbert and the rest of the posse regrouped to plan their next strategy. Finally, a decision was made to blow up the fort by placing sticks of dynamite at the foot of its foundation. This meant some crazy fool would have to make a run towards the fortress with no cover, dodging bullets, and return to the safety of the barricade under the same circumstances. This may be hard for some of us to understand, but the lawmen responsible for taming Indian Territory were cut from different cloth and did not like to say "no" to a challenge. Charlie Copeland, one of the engineers of the rolling barricade, instantly volunteered. Copeland had been wounded in an earlier battle with Christie and wanted to settle the score.

Sometime after midnight, Tolbert and Bill Smith stepped out to the right of the barricade and William Ellis and G. S. White stepped out to the left, rapidly firing their Winchesters at the fortress. This enabled Copeland to make a run for the south wall of the stronghold, then place and light six-inch sticks of dynamite. Despite having to dodge close-range rifle fire, the determined lawman was able to make it back to the safety of the barricade before the explosion, without being shot. The fuses quickly burned, igniting six sticks, blowing away the southern portion of the fortress and setting fire to what remained. The lawmen continued to take cover as splintered, burning logs from the cabin began falling back down to Earth around them.

The lawmen must have been awestruck at the sight of Ned's Fort Mountain lit-up by the remains of the burning, defeated fortress. When the debris settled, the five lawmen approached the burning remains, followed by the rest of the posse. Suddenly, to the surprise of the lawmen, the outlaws began firing at the posse from the fire. The outlaws had been hiding under the floor of the cabin when it exploded and were still very much alive and full of fight. As the posse encroached, the outlaws finally gave up their stand. The lawmen held their fire at first so as not to shoot fellow posse members. Arch Wolfe took advantage of the situation and was able to make a clean getaway. Charlie Hare held his ground until the fire became too much. He surrendered to lawmen after emerging badly burned from the inferno. Christie probably could have escaped that night, if his desire to kill had-

A dead Ned Christie with U.S. Marshals from Ft. Smith who killed him.
Photo credit: Western History Collections, University of Oklahoma Libraries.

n't gotten the best of him. He crawled from his burning fortress, got to his feet, and began to walk away. He crossed paths with a group of lawmen who mistook him for one of the posse. This could have been a chance to slip away quietly, but Christie couldn't resist such a close shot at his enemy. He raised his Winchester to his shoulder and fired so close to the lawmen's faces as to leave powder burns. The lawmen were otherwise unscathed and returned fire at the same close range. In a hail of gunfire, Christie sank to his knees, paused briefly, made a small sound, and pitched forward head first. Ned Christie was dead. After six years, Judge Parker's men finally ended the reign of the last great Cherokee warrior. Apparently the posse thought he might be playing possum, so they continued to fire at the lifeless corpse. Sam Maples, son of the murdered U.S. Deputy Marshal, was there to empty his revolver into the outlaw's lifeless body. During the battle, the posse had fired more than 2000 rounds of ammunition. The lawmen had fired 115 bullets into the dead outlaw.

The death of Ned Christie brought much relief to settlers around the

Tahlequah area. The body was brought to Fort Smith for the purpose of identification, allowing the lawmen to collect the rewards that had been offered by the government and private individuals. The outlaw's mangled body was propped upon a board in somewhat of a standing position by morbid citizens of Fort Smith as a warning to other territorial badmen. Christie's aforementioned model 1873 Winchester rifle was wired into his dead hands in a vain attempt to make him appear more animated. In the same manner a successful hunter might pose with a 16 point buck, members of the posse posed for pictures with the once great Cherokee warrior. On the evening of July 6, 1893, only a few months after the death of his father, Ned Christie's son James was attacked and killed by unknown assassins. His head was severed from his body, demonstrating just how hated his father was by some of the settlers in Indian Territory.

The January 9, 1896, issue of the *Vinita Leader* reported, "Bud Trainor, well-known here, was killed at Talala on Christmas night by four negroes. It was a plot and four shotguns did the work." Before his death, Trainor was part of a posse who attempted to arrest Christie. When Humphrey was 87-years-old, he said he wanted to set the record straight before he died. This is when he told his story to the *Daily Oklahoman* in 1918. He had been listed in court records as a witness in the murder case of Deputy Marshal Dan Maples.

Some will argue that no one actually knows who killed Marshal Maples. There is much to the Ned Christie story that cannot be confirmed. The remains of Ned's Fort Mountain are on private property near the town of Eldon, Oklahoma. Despite his crimes, Christie is revered by many as a great warrior who was a victim of bad luck and who fought a brave fight rather than surrender. Under different circumstances, Ned Christie might have been a great statesman and educator to his Cherokee people.

Chapter 5
Hell-Fire at Ingalls

Ingalls, Oklahoma is a small town in Payne County, about 35 miles northeast of Guthrie and 10 miles east of Stillwater. On September 1, 1893, it became known as the site of the most famous gunfight between lawmen and outlaws in Oklahoma history. Near Ingalls, the Doolin Gang frequented a campsite under a large overhang of rock along Deer Creek near the Cimarron River in the Creek Nation. To the southeast of Ingalls, about two and a half miles, was the homestead of Bill Dunn. The Dunn family aided and abetted the outlaw gang and gave them sanctuary when they were on the run. It was rumored the additions to the Dunn homestead were paid for with outlaw money. Bill Doolin, the gang's leader, quietly courted, then married a young lady from Ingalls, which was probably the main reason the gang hung around. Naturally, the residents of Ingalls became acquainted with members of the Doolin Gang. The boys were boisterous, sometimes shooting bottles off the bar with their .45 caliber revolvers. However the townspeople referred to the outlaws as likeable fellows. Most of the folks were partisan towards the gang members and alerted them to approaching lawmen. Some of the partisanship had been from fear of the outlaws, but there is no doubt the money the gang spent in the town made them very popular. Ingalls was not near a railroad and was not a boomtown, so naturally the local business community was happy to see cash-paying customers.

It didn't take long for Judge Parker's U.S. Deputy Marshals to learn about Ingalls. July 7, 1893, Deputy Marshal Tom Hueston of Stillwater and a posse man named Wilson rode into Ingalls to see what was afoot. As they attempted to dismount, they were confronted by members of the Doolin Gang and at gunpoint were instructed not to get off their horses. Since the outlaws had the advantage, the lawmen complied.

Both lawmen realized how lucky they were to be allowed to leave the town of Ingalls alive. Marshal Hueston quickly returned with a posse, but by then the outlaws had gone. The marshal may have taken personally the events of July 7 to the point where he would do something risky in order to settle his grudge with the Doolin Gang and the town of Ingalls. Regardless of his motivation, he was about to make a deadly mistake.

Lawmen were able to gather intelligence concerning the Doolin Gang due to a clever officer. Orrington "Red" Lucas, an officer of the Fort Smith Federal Court in Arkansas, posed as a poor fisherman to infiltrate the town of Ingalls. To make his cover complete, Lucas found as a partner a man named "Catfish Jack" he described as "the ugliest man in the territory." The two men put up an old tent in the town and went into the business of selling fish to the residents of Ingalls, including members of the Doolin Gang. After a hard day of work, the fishermen frequented one of the town's two saloons where they socialized and played cards with the outlaws. Another federal officer, W.C. "Doc" Roberts, had assimilated into the town and provided authorities with important information. On August 30, the two undercover officers delivered a detailed report to Deputy Marshal John W. Hixon of Guthrie.

Based on the information in the report, Marshal Hixon decided a good way to get the drop on the Doolin Gang would be to get two big wagons covered in white canvas, load them with men and ammunition, and drive them into town without drawing any attention. If anyone asked, they were to say they were hunters. Marshal Heck Thomas pronounced it a "fool's errand," and refused to have anything to do with it. Regardless of any dissension, the plan was put into action the night of August 31. Before midnight, a wagon left from Stillwater driven by Marshal Dick Speed under the command of Marshal Hueston and with Deputies "Ham" Hueston, the marshal's brother, Henry Keller, George Cox, M.A. Iauson and H.A. "Hi" Thompson. A little earlier, a wagon left from Guthrie driven by Marshal Jim Masterson under the command of Marshal Hixon and with Deputies Doc Roberts, Ike Steel, Steve Burke and Lafe Shadley.

The plan was for both wagons to meet with Red Lucas at his campsite. The lawmen then would circle the hotel and force the outlaws to surrender. Unfortunately for the lawmen, the wagon from Guthrie was delayed and didn't arrive until almost dawn. The lawmen had to improvise a plan "B," so Lucas was sent to town to gather intelligence. He returned around nine o'clock that morning to report that Bill Dalton, Bill Doolin, Tulsa Jack Blake, Dynamite Dick Clifton, Bitter Creek Newcomb and Red Buck Waightman were in

Ransom's Saloon, starting their day with whiskey and a few hands of poker. Arkansas Tom Jones had been in town, but said he wasn't feeling well and was thought to have gone to the Dunns.'

Marshal Hixon realized that even at odds of 13 lawmen against six members of the Doolin Gang, he was not guaranteed a victory. He dispatched a runner to Stillwater with orders for Chief Deputy Hale to assemble a posse and hightail it out here. The current challenge for the posse would be to keep the outlaws from leaving the town. Marshal Hixon ordered the two wagons to enter town from different points. Marshal Speed drove his wagon into Ingalls from the west and Marshal Masterson skirted his wagon along the outside of town and entered from the south on Oak Street. As the wagons entered the town, the lawmen, each armed with a Winchester rifle, two pistols and two belts of ammunition, dropped from under the canvas and took whatever cover they could find. The outlaws saw the first wagon skirt the side of town but weren't concerned until they saw the second, followed by their friend Lucas, drive down Ash Street and stop just past Light's Blacksmith Shop. The lawmen knew they had to prevent townsfolk from alerting the outlaws of their presence. Earlier, a young boy who had stumbled on to the posse's campsite was chained to a tree for safekeeping, after being interrogated by the officers. Marshal Speed slipped from the wagon on Ash and entered a feed barn, confronting liveryman Henry Pierce and 12-year-old stable boy Oscar Wagner. The marshal pointed his rifle at the two and, as Pierce later testified, "He told us he was a federal officer...that there was going to be some shooting, and if either of us tried to notify the outlaws, we'd be killed like dogs." Marshal Speed looked down the street to see Bitter Creek, whom he didn't recognize, walking his horse towards the wagon to investigate. Just then, seeing 14-year-old Dell Simmons step from Light's Blacksmith Shop, the marshal asked if he knew the man. The boy pointed at the man and said, "Why, that's Bitter Creek." At this point, the battle at Ingalls began. When Bitter Creek saw the boy point at him while talking to a stranger, he didn't ask any question, but threw his rifle to his shoulder. The marshal did likewise and managed to fire first, his round hitting the outlaw's rifle, knocking loose the magazine tube, and ricocheting into his right leg. The outlaw also fired, but his round went wild. He was unable to chamber a second cartridge with his damaged rifle, so he mounted his horse and turned around to ride out of town. The marshal was about to finish the outlaw when suddenly a rifle shot from the attic window of the hotel tore into his shoulder. It seemed Arkansas Tom had not gone to the Dunns,' but instead was resting in the attic room of the hotel. He heard a shot, then saw a man trying to kill his friend Bitter Creek, he grabbed his rifle and joined the fight. The marshal first started for the shelter of the stable, but decided instead to head for the wagon, which was a fatal mistake; Arkansas Tom shot him dead.

The unexpected gunfire caused the lawmen to join the fight before they had taken safe positions. The lawmen fired at Bitter Creek as he rode away, but by now the remaining outlaws in the saloon were alerted as well and fired at the lawmen enabling their partner to escape, still clutching his useless rifle. In the fusillade of gunfire, Dell Simmons and bar patron N.A. Walker were mortally wounded and died a few hours later. The two groups of lawmen concentrated on the saloon with Marshal Hueston's group covering the rear of the building and Marshal Hixon's group covering the front and the nearby livery stable. Marshal Hixon called out to the outlaws to surrender, informing them they were surrounded. Doolin eloquently replied, "Go to hell!"

Both groups of heavily armed lawmen spent the next few minutes ventilating Ransom's Saloon as the outlaws returned fire. The gang was outgunned and outmanned; the only chance they had was to make a break for the livery stable, and ride like hell out of town. The lawmen were unaware of the side door the outlaws used to escape. To divert attention from their departure, Neil D. Murray foolishly stood by the open front door of the saloon with a rifle as if he intended to fire. For his effort, Murray was struck by one round that broke his arm and another two striking his ribs. Old man Ransom was already wounded from a round to the leg. The lawmen were reportedly unaware the saloon had been vacated until they were fired upon from the livery stable. The outlaws fired at the lawmen while they planned their escape.

At the point where the battle moved to the livery stable, a story began involving "Rose of the Cimarron." As the story goes, upon seeing her outlaw lover, wounded and low on ammunition, she tied together bed sheets and climbed down from a hotel window with guns and cartridges. When the gun battle was at its height, she heroically ran to the aid of her lover forsaking the flying lead all around her. The truth is there was a young teenaged girl named Rosa Dunn who was part of the Dunn family who harbored the outlaws. She was a beautiful girl with dark hair who was familiar with the outlaws, but was not involved in the battle at Ingalls.

The lawmen had to move from their positions to better cover the livery stable. The posse thought they were no longer accessible to the sniper in the hotel attic, but they didn't know Arkansas Tom had punched a hole through the shingles of the roof and was standing on a chair to command a bird's eye view of the battle. Marshal Tom Hueston took cover behind a woodpile which put him where the lone outlaw could put two rounds into his left side. As he crumpled, he said, "I'd like to see the man who shot me." Inside the livery stable, Doolin and Dynamite Dick saddled the horses while Dalton, Tulsa Jack and Red Buck fired at the lawmen. Suddenly, the back and front doors of the barn flew open and the outlaws on their horses made a mad dash in two directions. Doolin and Dynamite Dick rode out the back of the stable to the southwest and Dalton, Tulsa Jack and Red Buck stampeded out the front. The latter three had to ride past the guns of the posse to the safety of a ravine just a few hundred yards in front of them. Dalton's horse took a round in the jaw, but the outlaw managed to regain control of his mount which he rode another 75 yards when another round broke the animal's leg. Dalton fell with his horse and tumbled, but was unhurt. He took off running to catch up with the other outlaws only to find their way blocked by a wire fence and realizing the only pair of wire cutters were in Dalton's saddle bags on his injured horse. Dalton ran back towards his horse, encountering Marshal Lafe Shadley. The outlaw fired at the lawman but missed. As Marshal Shadley ran for cover and tried to get through a wire fence, his hip was shattered by a round from Arkansas Tom's rifle.

Memorial of U.S. Marshals Dick Speed, Tom Houston, and Lafe Shadley.
*Photo credit: Archives & Manuscripts Division
of the Oklahoma Historical Society.*

Dalton grabbed his wire cutters, put his horse out of its misery, and returned to the gang and cut the fence. The injured lawman made it to the house of Mrs. Ransom who refused to offer any assistance. She told the lawman to go to a nearby cave where several people were already hiding. As the two debated, Marshal Shadley was shot a second time, forcing him to crawl to the cave. The dying lawman thought he had been shot by Dalton, but the angle of the bullets indicated he had been shot from above.

The outlaws cleared the fence and rode to the southeast, pausing at the top of a hill to fire a volley of shots down Ash Street. Dr. Briggs' teenage son Frank ran to an intersection to see the excitement and was shot in the shoulder.

Chief Deputy Hale arrived with the posse from Stillwater and trailed the outlaw gang. The first posse didn't have horses to chase the fleeing gang, so they concentrated on the sniper in the hotel. The lawmen fired continuously at the attic and roof of the hotel. Arkansas Tom, for awhile, fired back. By 11 o'clock a.m., the lawmen realized this effort was futile. Once again, they demanded Jones give himself up, to which he responded, "If I come out, I'll come shooting!"

Here again, we come to a segment of the Ingalls' tale that has been obscured by early writers with a flair for the dramatic. As the legend goes, the posse either planted dynamite around the hotel or piled brush for burning, then threatened to destroy the building. Mrs. Pierce pleaded with the lawmen, saying the hotel was her only source of income. As a last resort, Mrs. Pierce was allowed one last attempt to talk the outlaw into surrendering. The lady went upstairs to plead her case to the outlaw, who was so chivalrous he surrendered to authorities rather than be the source of such an inconvenience.

In Glenn Shirley's book *West of Hell's Fringe* (University of Oklahoma Press, 1978), he cites the diary of Dr. D. R. Pickering who was present during the battle and who talked to Arkansas Tom before his surrender. According to the doctor, he had gone to the hotel and called up to Jones to see if he were all right. The outlaw said he wanted to talk, so the doctor walked upstairs to see him. Jones asked the doctor where the other outlaws were holed-up. The doctor described

Close up of plaque on monument.
Photo credit: Archives & Manuscripts Division of the Oklahoma Historical Society.

in his diary the outlaw's reaction upon learning the gang had left him, "He said he did not think they would leave him it hurt him bad I never seen a man wilt so in my life. He staid (sic) in hotel till after 2 o'clock and then surrendered to a Mr. Mason, a preacher."

The battle was over. Chief Deputy Hale's posse lost the outlaws' trail when the gang crossed over into the Sac and Fox Nation. Arkansas Tom was taken to Stillwater and locked in the Payne County jail. Marshal Dick Speed was dead and Marshals Tom Hueston and Lafe Shadley were mortally wounded, dying a few hours later in Stillwater. The marshals were all good men who had many friends in the community who were outraged. Angry men formed amateur posses that attempted to trail the outlaw gang but, predictably, and luckily, had no success. One only can imagine the result of average citizens' waging war on a gang of professional badmen.

Keeping Arkansas Tom in the Stillwater jail became a problem. There were rumors that townspeople were going to break into the jail and lynch him, in addition to rumors of the Doolin Gang's riding in to rescue their friend and burn the town. Arkansas Tom was transferred to the jail in Guthrie, however, so were the threats. Marshals Hixon and Thomas organized two groups totaling 40 men to patrol the town of Guthrie. They were backed up by the citizens who promised to repeat the events at Coffeyville should the outlaws enter their town.

There were three marshals and two citizens of Ingalls dead. Two men and a boy were seriously wounded and the town of Ingalls had been shot full of holes. For all their effort, the lawmen had wounded Bitter Creek in the leg, Dynamite Dick in the neck and arrested a 19-year-old boy who ran out of ammunition.

Arkansas Tom Jones was tried for murder, but with all the flying lead that day, proving who shot whom was no easy task. There was no conclusive proof, but the presumption of guilt was strong enough for a conviction. Due to these extenuating circumstances, Jones was not hanged, but sentenced to 50 years in the federal penitentiary in Leavenworth, Kansas. Jones had two brothers who were ministers and who lobbied for his release. Due to their efforts, Arkansas Tom was pardoned after serving only 14 years. He went straight for several years, but the temptation must have been too great; he was re-sentenced to prison after being involved in a bank robbery at Neosho, Missouri. Upon his release, Jones robbed a bank in Asbury, Missouri, on August 16, 1924, but by then his luck had ran out; he was killed while resisting arrest. This made Arkansas Tom Jones the longest surviving member of the Doolin Gang.

There may have been no winners after the battle at Ingalls, but it did help turn the tide of popular opinion against the Doolin Gang. They were no longer viewed as glamorous and daring, but as killers who ended the lives of three good men rather than face the music of their deeds. The members of the Doolin Gang did receive their comeuppance; some saw prison, most saw hell.

The town of Ingalls still exists today. Visitors pay their respects to the marshals killed during the town's famous battle at a monument erected in their honor. Their spirit and bravery will not be forgotten.

Chapter 6
Cattle Annie and Little Britches

No book about Oklahoma outlawry would be complete without mention of Annie McDoulet and Jennie Stevens, better known as Cattle Annie and Little Britches (usually pronounced "Breeches"). Both girls were juvenile delinquents who fell in with a bad crowd–the infamous Doolin Gang. Their crimes included bootlegging and horse theft earning them stiffer than usual sentences. This was due in part to their gang affiliation, but also because of their own well-deserved notoriety. Although they may have appeared as a couple of moppets, these two girls in their early teens proved to outlaws and lawmen alike they were tough enough to run with the big dogs.

Cattle Annie (Anna McDoulet) and Little Britches (Jennie Stevens) first met members of the Doolin Gang at a country dance. The girls soon became spies for the gang and let them know when lawmen were in the area. The outlaws must have been very exciting to a couple of young girls who only knew life on their parents' farms near the town of Red Rock.

Early accounts referred to the girls' parents as poor, but respectable farmers from Indian Territory. However, in the case of the McDoulets, there is more to the story. James Clemens McDoulet, Annie's father, was described as both "a preacher-lawyer from Fall River, Kansas, who was in poor circumstances when he moved to Skiatook, Indian Territory" and then later as "an attorney and esteemed justice in the town of Red Rock." He and his wife, Rebecca Jane, raised seven sons and three daughters, including Anna. Both families were repeatedly referred to as respectable.

Annie and Jennie worked as domestics during the day, and at night met with their partners in crime. These two young girls who rode with outlaws were much more liberated than other young girls in the 1890s. They dared to wear men's pants and ride their horses "astride" instead of "sidesaddle" as was the fashion for ladies. It wasn't unusual for women living in Indian Territory to be armed. However, it was usually with smaller guns that better fit their hands; such was not the case with Cattle Annie and Little Britches. To top off their rough and ready appearance, they wore full-size six-shooters in their gun belts that were also equipped with cartridges, just like the other members of the gang. The girls were also in possession of

Cattle Annie and Little Britches 61

Anna McDoulet, alias Cattle Annie, and Jennie Stevens, alias Little Britches. *Photo credit: Archives & Manuscripts Division of the Oklahoma Historical Society.*

Winchester rifles and were reputed to be crack-shots.

The girls had met the outlaws towards the demise of the Doolin Gang. As the badmen were dispersed and killed by marshals, the girls went their own way. Cattle Annie stayed in the area while Little Britches endured two short, unsuccessful attempts at marriage. Before long, the two hooked up again and reverted to their old habits which included bootlegging and stealing horses. Both girls had been arrested by local lawmen at different times. Annie had been released on bond and left the area. Jennie also had been in police custody, but made a break for it after eating her dinner at a local hotel in the presence of lawmen. She jumped on a horse, rode out of town with the lawmen on her heels, and eluded her pursuers into the night.

The girls' crimes could be considered petty when compared to more violent acts of outlawry that occurred in Indian Territory, but the two attracted the attention of Judge Parker's U.S. Deputy Marshals. Lawmen knew of their association with the Doolin Gang and were soon hot on their trail. In 1895, U.S. Deputy Marshals Steve Burke and Bill Tilghman trailed the girls to a farmhouse near Pawnee. As the lawmen approached the dwelling, Little Britches ran out through the back, mounted her horse and rode off like a shot. Tilghman followed in quick pursuit, leaving Burke to contend with Cattle Annie. The lawman approached the farmhouse with caution. Creeping along an outside wall, he attempted to look inside an open window. At the same moment, Cattle Annie peered out the window from the other side, armed with a Winchester. The two surprised each other. Before Annie could wield her rifle, Marshal Burke grabbed her by the shoulders and pulled her outside through the window. Having lost her rifle, the outlaw attempted to pull her pistol as soon as her feet hit the ground, however Burke was able to disarm her and make the arrest.

Marshal Tilghman was experiencing challenges of his own. His thoroughbred was in much better shape than Jennie's old nag and had no trouble catching up with the outlaw. The next few events exemplified beyond any doubt the chivalrous character of Bill Tilghman. In desperation, the bad girl fired at the lawman from over her shoulder, but was not accustomed to riding and shooting, so her shots went wild. Tilghman could not bring himself to shoot back at a woman, so he continued to chase his quarry while dodging bullets. Although Tilghman was long on chivalry, his patience was coming to an end. Woman or not, he still had an obligation to apprehend the fleeing fugitive. The lawman drew his rifle and shot Jennie's horse dead, sending rider and carcass for a tumble. Her leg was trapped under her mount which prevented her both from escaping and from reaching her gun only inches away. Tilghman confronted a wildcat who was cursing while she clawed at the ground towards her gun. The lawman picked up her revolver, emptied it, then helped the young girl get herself free. The spunky outlaw came up fighting, throwing a handful of dirt into the lawman's eyes. Despite her best efforts to resist, Little Britches was finally under arrest. When the marshals met back at the farmhouse, Tilghman's eyes were still stinging and Burke had a long scratch across his cheek, but the lawmen had their prisoners. The criminal careers of Anna McDoulet and Jennie Stevens had ended, but the legend of Cattle Annie and Little Britches was about to begin.

Early September, 1895, Anna McDoulet and Jennie Stevens were tried in Pawnee. They had been cleaned up and dressed to appear as sweet, innocent young ladies. Early accounts of their courtroom antics described how they "shouted" at the judge and attorneys, referred to the lawmen as "soft" and boasted of their affiliation with the Doolin Gang. This is probably because of an anonymous article appearing in the April 16, 1939, issue of *The Guthrie Daily Leader*. According to Glenn Shirley's book *West of Hell's Fringe* (University of Oklahoma Press, 1978), this was only part of the Cattle Annie and Little Britches legend. Actually, the girls were seemingly at a loss for words. Jennie sulked and Annie spoke only to say she had been raised right, but was past redemption and would resume her outlaw life.

Anna McDoulet was sent to a reform school at South Framingham, Massachusetts. Jennie Stevens was found guilty of horse stealing and was sentenced to two years in a reformatory prison in Sherborn, Massachusetts, but was first taken to Guthrie to face an old charge of selling whiskey in Indian Territory. With the judge convinced of her desire to change, the charges were dismissed and Jennie was sent to Sherborn to serve her sentence. She was released in October of 1896 after only one year due to the efforts of her family. Jennie returned to her father's home near Sinnett in Pawnee County. She began a life of quiet obscurity, expressing regret for her transgressions and claiming to be completely reformed. Little Britches faded into legend; Jennie Stevens, however, married and settled down with her husband in the Tulsa area where she raised a fine family. Two years after having been sent "back East," Cattle Annie was supposed to have died of "consumption" (tuberculosis) in a New York hospital. In a way, she did. According to an article appearing in the April, 1997, issue of *True West* Magazine, Anna McDoulet quietly returned to Indian Territory and on March 13, 1901, married a man named Earl Frost in Perry. In October of 1909, Anna divorced and had joined the "101 Wild West Show." She later remarried and settled with her husband in Oklahoma City. After her death in 1978, she was buried in Oklahoma City.

Cattle Annie and Little Britches were a couple of colorful characters from Indian Territory. Anna McDoulet and Jennie Stevens, however, were a couple of juvenile delinquents who, because of the company they kept, were given severe sentences they may not have deserved. After the girls paid their debts to society, they returned home, thankful for the second chance they had been given.

Chapter 7
A Badman Whose Word Was Good

Bill Doolin had enough of Indian Territory. His friends Bitter Creek Newcomb and Charley Pierce had been killed, marking the end of his once feared outlaw gang. Hiding out and living life on the run was different when the gang was together, but the law had shut down the store on the Doolin Gang. The Dover Train robbery (see chapter three) had been the end of the line for Doolin's gang. The game was over; it was time to get out of the outlaw business.

Bill Doolin was born in 1858 in Johnson County, Arkansas. He grew up on his family's farm, learning the duties and responsibilities necessary for survival in a rural area. These talents included working with livestock and using a rifle to put wild game on the table. These were also two talents one could rely on to successfully trail cattle through Indian Territory.

In 1881, Doolin headed west to find employment and the cattle ranchers were pleased to have the hardworking lanky youth as a hand. He became a bit of a rambler, riding wherever the cattle business took him. By 1891, he was working at the Bar X Bar Ranch near Arkansas City, Kansas. During a three-day Fourth of July celebration in Coffeyville, Bill Doolin went from "good ol' boy" to outlaw.

Not far from the July Fourth celebration, in a wooded area, was a more "spirited" get-together involving a group of young cowboys. Despite strict prohibition laws in Kansas, the group was in possession of half-barrels filled with bottled beer and ice, as well as at least one beer keg. Before long, a couple of constables learned of the party and hurried to put an end to it. They walked up on the beer bust and demanded to know who owned the contraband; this was one time when Doolin should have stifled his natural predisposition for leadership. He informed the officers that no one owned the beer and there was no charge to drink. The officers declared they were going to confiscate the beer which made the cowboys very excited; enough so that a shoot-out followed and the two constables were seriously wounded. Since Doolin spoke up, he was assigned blame as group leader and was outlawed ever since.

As happens with men on the dodge, they tended to fall in with people of like circumstances. Doolin soon became a member of the infamous Dalton Gang which had one goal as outlaws – to surpass the former James/Younger Gang in deeds and reputation. The Daltons mainly robbed trains, but did at least once contemplate bank robbery. Doolin had tasted the outlaw life and wanted more.

It was by accident that Doolin was not involved in the disastrous, double bank robbery at Coffeyville, Kansas, when his horse came up lame. After the robbery, Bob Dalton, Grat Dalton, Dick Broadwell and Bill Powers were killed, and Emmett Dalton was wounded and placed under arrest. Once again, Doolin's leadership skills put him as the leader of what would become the Doolin Gang. They had a fairly successful run, until the April 3, 1895 Dover train robbery which marked the beginning of the gang's end. The next day, Tulsa Jack Blake was killed by a posse during the Cimarron River shoot-out. About a month later, Charley Pierce and Bitter Creek Newcomb would be killed by lawmen at the Dunn Ranch near Ingalls. Three of Doolin's friends going back to his "Dalton days" were now dead and the rest were scattered. Without his pals, there was no reason to stay around Indian Territory with the law hot on his trail.

Doolin had met a young girl who worked at a store in Ingalls. Over the course of a year, he secretly courted, then married Edith Ellsworth in 1894. By the time of the Dover train robbery, the couple had a one-year-old son. By early 1896, Doolin was ready to settle down with his family and enjoy the simple life. When Doolin began his life as an outlaw, he was a strong young man in his early-30s. However, five years of life on the run had taken its toll on the once spry youth. Due to hard living and a wound from a .30/30 round to his right foot, the outlaw was now a man crippled with rheumatism and looking at 40. Edith Doolin (or Ellsworth as she was still known) and her baby lived with her family and could meet with her outlaw husband only in secret. Mr. and Mrs. Doolin passed each other messages through Mrs. Pierce who owned the hotel in Ingalls (see chapter five). Doolin was hiding out in New Mexico with friends while his attorney attempted to negotiate a plea bargain with authorities that would allow the outlaw to plead guilty to reduced charges and receive only a light sentence. Doolin's attorney met with Marshal E.D. Nix at least three times, explaining how his client had not killed anyone and was being blamed for some robberies in which he did not participate. Marshal Nix was unmoved, explaining how the outlaw's reign had gone for too long. Attempting to arrest Doolin and his gang had resulted in the deaths of too many lawmen. Marshal Nix had spent from his own pocket more than $2,000 in addition to the tens of thousands spent by the government in tracking Doolin and his friends. There was no deal to be made. The marshals would find Doolin and make him pay.

 U.S. Deputy Marshal Bill Tilghman was the most celebrated lawman in Oklahoma History. Tilghman, along with Marshals Chris Madsen and Heck Thomas, was one of the "Three Guardsmen" who were responsible for the arrests of more than 300 outlaws. Marshal Tilghman had received a tip that Doolin had traveled to Eureka Springs, Arkansas. It was here the outlaw found temporary relief from his crippling rheumatism at hot bath resorts. Usually, in a situation where a dangerous outlaw is located, a group of lawmen would make the capture to ensure success. Marshal Tilghman could have, though a large posse might spook his quarry. Maybe he just wanted the glory of a dynamic, single-handed capture. There has been much speculation and myth concerning Doolin's arrest by Marshal Tilghman some promoted by the marshal, himself.

 One popular myth is that Marshal Tilghman stopped by the Dunn Ranch looking for the Doolin Gang. The outlaws were hiding in a dugout while they watched the marshal ask questions of Mr. Dunn. As the marshal was walking away, the notorious Red Buck Waightman wanted to shoot him in the back. Doolin warned his fellow badman not to do the deed, because Marshal Tilghman was too good of a man to be shot in the back. A few days later, the marshal learned of his close call and felt so indebted to the outlaw that he vowed to bring him in alive. The story came from a pamphlet entitled *The Passing of the Oklahoma Outlaws*, written by Richard S. Graves.

William Tilghman
*Photo credit: Archives & Manuscripts Division
of the Oklahoma Historical Society.*

The pamphlet was distributed during a historical photo-drama being presented throughout the southwest by Bill Tilghman. According to Tilghman, he arrived in Eureka Springs, Arkansas on a Wednesday, January 15, 1896. He immediately spotted Doolin, who he soon learned was staying at the Davy Hotel under the name of Tom Wilson, an alias he had used before. The lawman devised what seemed like an elaborate plan when compared to the simplicity of the actual arrest. He had instructed a local carpenter to build a wooden box in which a shotgun could be concealed and quickly retrieved when the outlaw was encountered. In the meantime, the road-weary marshal decided to freshen up in the mineral water of a local bathhouse. As he stepped into the gentlemen's waiting room of the bathhouse, he saw Bill Doolin on a lounge chair reading a paper. Some earlier publications of this account stated that Doolin had not recognized the lawman because he was disguised as a "preacher."

Marshal Tilghman turned his face from Doolin and took up a position where he could observe the outlaw while unseen. The marshal wasn't sure if he had been noticed by the outlaw. If he had, there would have been no second chance in this town to make an arrest. The marshal unholstered his revolver and walked up to the outlaw who was still reading his paper. He pointed his gun at Doolin and ordered him to throw up his hands and surrender. A startled Doolin snapped back that he hadn't done anything, as he slipped his right hand under his vest. The marshal grabbed Doolin's right sleeve with his free left hand to prevent the outlaw from pulling his revolver from his shoulder holster. When the gunplay started, the waiting room crowded with startled bathhouse patrons took about 30 seconds to empty, allowing the two their privacy. Doolin continued to struggle for his pistol, but the marshal convinced him it was certain death; Doolin surrendered. Marshal Tilghman, with both hands full, summoned the bathhouse owner to disarm Doolin. The outlaw persisted he had done nothing. The marshal knew how to talk to men in terms of threats and reason. He explained to Doolin that they were in country where an outlaw, especially one as notorious as he, ran the risk of being lynched if people knew who he was. The captured outlaw realized the best thing to do would be to get on the train for Guthrie with the marshal and take his chances in court.

Here is the part of the tale that makes it so special. Marshal Tilghman cuffed his prisoner, then reconsidered. He told Doolin that he would remove his irons, if he would give his word to "go along all right." The most desperate, dangerous outlaw in the whole territory could have exploited this situation to plot an escape, but he didn't. Bill Doolin was an old-time cowboy who knew how to ride, shoot straight and speak the truth. Even as a wanted outlaw, Doolin had standards. As one story goes, he banished Red Buck Waightman from his gang after he shot and killed an unarmed preacher in order to steal his horse. The outraged Doolin brought his gang to a halt so the money from their last job could be divided. He threw Red Buck his cut and said, "Now you get out! You're too damn low to associate with a high-class gang of train robbers."

Whether the exchange between Doolin and Red Buck happened or not, it's a great story. Marshal Tilghman knew these qualities of Doolin were real and that if the outlaw gave his word, he meant it. The outlaw agreed to the marshal's terms and was allowed to walk like a free man, in the marshal's company, to his hotel room to collect his belongings. The two men rode on the train back to Guthrie just like a couple of old chums, chatting and laughing. Of course, one fact that can not be overlooked is that if the lame, unarmed outlaw tried to make a break for it, the armed lawman would shoot him dead.

On January 16, what seemed like the whole town of Guthrie, and then some, came to the train depot to catch a glimpse of the notorious badman. At this stage of the game, Doolin wasn't looking like the stuff of legend. Marshal Tilghman stepped off the train with a tall, skinny man who wore a droopy mustache and walked with a cane. The town of Guthrie was still fascinated. After the outlaw was locked in the new jail, a reception line of about 1000 people filed through the building so they could tell the generations to come that they had met the famous Oklahoma Outlaw Bill Doolin.

Bill Doolin was indeed a man of his word. He promised Marshal Tilghman that he would come along and not make a break from him.

Only now, Doolin was no longer in the custody of Marshal Tilghman. He hadn't promised these lawmen a thing.

Doolin had been locked in the new federal jail in Guthrie. Because of the building's design, it was considered to be a safe place to keep dangerous federal prisoners. However, a jail is only as good as the people running it.

Doolin was happy to see one of his old gang members, Dynamite Dick Clifton, who was being housed in the same building. With a new jail full of hard-core badmen, it was only a matter of time before a security flaw would be exploited.

It was Sunday night, July 5, 1896, when one of the two jailers was seized through the bars by prisoners and had his gun ripped from its shoulder holster. Before the second jailer could close the door, Doolin ran through and grabbed the other jailer's gun that was in a box just outside of the cells. Eight prisoners, including Bill Doolin and Dynamite Dick, broke out of the Guthrie jail disrupting the usual serenity of a quiet summer's night.

The two jailers were fired for incompetence and manhunts were organized to round up the escapees. Marshal Heck Thomas knew where he could find Doolin because of an old strategy used by lawmen called "find the woman." The outlaw's wife and child were residing with her parents in Lawson, OK, presently the town of Quay, along the border of Pawnee and Payne Counties. It was a sure bet Doolin would collect them and leave the territory. Marshal Thomas and his posse rode to Lawson and staked out the area around the Reverend Ellsworth's grocery store, which was next to his home. On the night of August 24, the marshal and his posse were waiting outside when Doolin left the house with a rifle and a pistol. He had heard something outside and thought it was some local children come to spy on him. The outlaw didn't want an audience and was going to scare them away. As Doolin walked down the road, lawmen on both sides of him told him to throw up his hands. Doolin fired towards one voice then the other, but he couldn't see his targets, unlike the lawmen who drew bull's-eyes. A blast from an eight-gauge shotgun peppered the outlaw's upper torso with at least 20 buckshot, four tearing through his heart. When the shooting stopped,

A Badman Whose Word Was Good 73

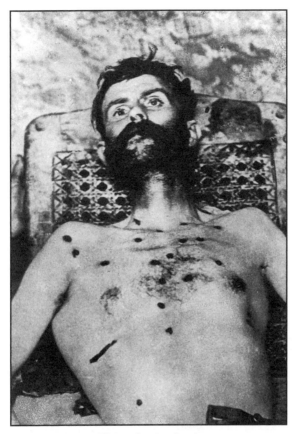

Bill Doolin, in death.
*Photo credit: Western History Collections,
University of Oklahoma Libraries*

a heartbroken Edith Doolin ran to her fallen husband as the sympathetic lawmen watched quietly. The outlaw career of Bill Doolin had come to an end.

Marshal Thomas received $1,425 in reward for ending Doolin's reign. Some of the money was redistributed in varied amounts to members of the posse. When Doolin escaped from custody, Marshal Tilghman lost claim to any reward and received nothing for his efforts.

Partisans of Doolin started a rumor that the outlaw had died from natural causes. It was claimed that the posse, after making a deal with Mrs. Doolin, leaned the corpse against a tree and shot it so they could

Tombstone of William "Bill" Doolin located at the
Summit View Cemetery in Guthrie, Oklahoma.
Photo credit: Author

collect the reward. An autopsy and overwhelming firsthand testimony soon put the rumor to rest. Bill Doolin was buried at Summit View Cemetery in Guthrie, Oklahoma. Originally, a twisted, rusty buggy-axle was used to mark the outlaw's resting place. If you visit the grave today, a large, red headstone marks the spot in the cemetery's "boot hill." The final monument, to an unforgettable outlaw.

Chapter 8
Christians From Hell

On June 30, 1895, the notorious Christian Brothers and Jim Casey staged a daring, daylight escape from the Oklahoma County Jail in Oklahoma City. When the smoke cleared, one lawman and one prisoner were dead.

Bill and Bob Christian were a couple of hard-luck outlaws who led a gang of small-time thieves and whiskey peddlers. The Christian Brothers ran wild around the Sacred Heart area in Pottawatomie County where they were raised and lived with their parents. This was a wild, wide open area where liquor was legally sold; on the other side of the border in Indian Territory it was prohibited. Regardless of where the liquor ended up being sold, Pottawatomie County boasted two licensed distilleries and 62 saloons. Dangerous towns like Keokuk Falls (see chapter ten) and Violet Springs sprang up along the border of Indian Territory where there was no law and violent crimes were the order of the day. Since only the most major crimes attracted the attention of lawmen, the Christian Brothers' petty crimes went mostly uninvestigated. Their luck ran out when a mercantile owned by John F. Brown, Governor of the Seminole Nation, reported a major loss of merchandise. The Christian Brothers were former employees and were immediately suspected, resulting in an arrest warrant being issued for Bob Christian on a charge of grand larceny.

On a Saturday morning, April 27, 1895, Deputy Sheriff Will Turner caught up with the outlaw. Bob Christian was in the company of brother Bill and a couple of their cronies, Foster Holbrook and "Buttermilk" John Mackey, in a small grove near Violet Springs. Deputy Turner informed Bob he had a warrant for his arrest to which he replied, "Damn you, you'd better keep it." Bob went for his gun, but the deputy drew first and fired, hitting the outlaw square in his breast from less than a yard away. Bob must have been wearing a steel breast plate because he fell, appeared stunned for a moment, then all four outlaws pulled their pistols and cut the lawman down in a hail of bullets. Holbrook and Mackey were arrested the next day by a posse led by Pottawatomie County Sheriff W.B. (Billy) Trousdale. The Christian Brothers went on the lam until May 22, when they turned themselves in to face the charges. It seems that Judge Scott must have believed there was something to Bob's claim of self-defense. Holbrook was acquitted, Mackey received a two-year sentence for manslaughter in the second degree. Instead of being found guilty of murder, Bob and Bill Christian each received a 10-year sentence for first-degree manslaughter.

On June 10, the Christian Brothers were transferred to the county jail in Oklahoma City, pending an appeal. In their cell block, they met James Casey, who was awaiting trial for murdering a deputy in Yukon. The trio soon began plotting their escape. Friends of the Christians, Bill's girlfriend and the boys' own father conspired to smuggle the prisoners guns and ammunition. The evening of June 30, at 6:30, Casey and the Christians removed three .45 caliber revolvers from a stovepipe in their cell and waited for the jailer.

J.H. Garver entered the corridor to lock the prisoners in their cells when he was surprised by three armed men. After a slight struggle, the three outlaws left the jail and ran south down an alley. Seventy-five feet from the jail door was Chief of Police Milt Jones' horse, tied in the alley. In the spirit of "every man for himself," Bill Christian ran down the alley, mounted the horse and left his partners. Just like a modern day commuter, he rode down Broadway, then turned to the west, riding through an alley between California and Reno. Having cleared the town, he rode away heading southwest.

Casey and the remaining Christian ran down Grand Avenue. As they approached Broadway, they unsuccessfully tried to commandeer a horse-drawn buggy. Chief Jones was on Broadway by the corner of Grand and came to intervene in the "buggy-jacking" with his gun drawn. Bob Christian stepped from the buggy and shot the police chief, mortally wounding him. By now, other lawmen had come to aid in the fight and began firing at the outlaws, the buggy and the innocent man and woman who were riding in it. Casey was killed almost instantly, shot through the neck and just above the ear. Mr. White, who was riding in the buggy, was shot in the leg and the abdomen with three more bullets tearing through his clothes; his passenger, Mrs. Hurt, was unscathed. Christian took off running down

Grand Avenue with a volley of gunfire chasing him. The lawmen knew at least one of the rounds must have hit, because his face appeared bloody. It was later learned the outlaw had been shot through the fleshy part of his neck. Undaunted, the bloody, desperate fugitive ran past the railroad tracks to encounter another chance to strong-arm transportation. It must have been a terrifying sight for blacksmith Frank Berg, as a desperate man, his face dripping with blood and sweat, pointed his gun and commanded him to jump from his wagon. Berg obliged and Christian whipped the horse into top speed, heading east, then south over the North Canadian River. On the other side, he took off to the east with a posse about 600 feet behind him. The woods were searched despite the sun's going down. Christian's trail led to the river bank where the lawmen concluded he must have drowned because of his wounds.

Back in Oklahoma City, authorities were wondering what had happened. It seemed sure that all the company the Christian Brothers had received in the last week was part of the plot, but authorities were in for a surprise.

The loss of Chief of Police Milt Jones had much impact on the Oklahoma City community. He was a first-rate lawman and friend; for many, their grief turned to frustration. Blame was laid on Garver for being negligent in his duties as a jailer.

On the evening of July 12, two of the conspirators were arrested by deputies near Violet Springs. Jessie Findlay, one of the pair arrested, was Bill Christian's girlfriend who had posed as the boys' sister when visiting the jail. She confirmed the lax conditions of the county jail and how easy it was for her and the others to supply the inmates with ammunition and three .45 caliber revolvers. Jessie also described the three guns used in the breakout; two had black handles and one had a fancy white handle decorated with an eagle's head. This was the same gun used to kill Deputy Turner that Bob Christian handed to Deputies Carr and Watts when he and his brother surrendered to authorities. Sheriff Trousdale was soon able to make a direct connection between Deputy Bill Carr and the men who smuggled the guns into the jail. He learned of a meeting between two members of the gang named Reeves and Fessenden, and Deputy Carr in a house southeast of Tahlequah. This is where the deputy gave the two men Bob Christian's pistol. Deputy Carr then wired the Oklahoma County jail that he believed the brothers were planning an escape. Garver, the jailer, admitted he received the telegram on November 27, but thought it to be a fake, so he never bothered to inform anyone else. When Reeves was captured, he also claimed that Deputy Carr had known all about plans for a jailbreak. Deputy Marshal Bill Carr was indicted by the grand jury, but while awaiting trial, he disappeared, not to be heard from again. It was rumored he became a captain in the insurgent army of Cuba and may have been killed in battle, but no one knows for sure. Garver was indicted for carelessly permitting the prisoners to escape. He was found guilty and sentenced to 10 years. He was released after two years, then died shortly after.

The grand jury indicted a couple of non-lawmen, but they were never brought to trial.

Bob Christian did not drown in the North Canadian River on the night of the jailbreak. Using a log for a floatation device, he floated downstream for several miles. Two days later, he reached his home in Pottawatomie County, where he stayed with neighbors who patched his neck wound. After a week, Bob was strong enough to ride off and join his brother.

After stealing Jones' horse, Bill Christian rode east, eluding his pursuers along the Little River. By July 8, the Christian Brother were reunited. They made plans to assemble a first-rate group of outlaws, wreaking vengeance on their enemies and rivaling any deeds of the Dalton Gang; but it didn't quite work out that way. After a few non-spectacular robberies that did little more than draw the attention of the law, the Christian Brothers and their father, referred to as "Old Man Christian," moved west to New Mexico, then to Arizona, never to return to Oklahoma.

In 1896, a couple of cowboys calling themselves Frank "Black Jack" Williams and Tom Anderson settled in the Arizona area and began working for local cattle companies. As men experienced in the cattle business, they found steady employment and were able to make a good living. The men often mentioned how it would be more profitable to assemble a gang to rob trains. As it turned out, Black Jack Williams was actually Bill Christian and Tom Anderson was his brother Bob. By July of 1896, they had assembled a gang and taken the name of a popular card game, calling themselves the "High Fives."

The gang robbed banks, post offices, and stores, never letting a posse get too close. In April of 1897, Bill Christian was killed in an ambush by lawmen along the Cole Creek near Clifton, Arizona. Bob operated the gang for a few months thereafter, until November 25 when he was arrested after a brawl in Chihuahua, Mexico. On December 9, before he could be extradited back to America, he escaped from jail and rode off into obscurity, never to be heard from again.

Were the Christian Brothers truly bad guys or just rambunctious young men who grew up in a rough and dangerous place? Many people in Indian Territory looked to the James, Dalton and Doolin Gangs as role models and to some, their goals became to surpass their deeds. It seems that the most impressive thing the Christian Brothers ever did was escape from the Oklahoma County Jail. However we now know this was only accomplished because of incompetence and corruption. Regardless of the reason, the Christian Brothers became a notorious part of the history of Oklahoma.

Chapter 9
The Reign of Terror in the Osage Hills

Oklahoma is a land known for its colorful past. When people think of Oklahoma history, they tend to remember moments such as the land runs or statehood that make one proud to be an Oklahoman. The fact is, there were dark periods in Sooner State history that included prejudice, corruption, injustice and murder. These are words describing the events that have come to be known as the "Reign of Terror in the Osage Hills." Early in the classic James Stewart movie *The F.B.I. Story*, there is a recreation of these events. During this segment of the movie, the most memorable scene is of a house being blown up, killing the family and their housekeeper; this really happened! In fact, this movie closely depicts the crimes committed against the Osage Indians, going as far as to use the real names of some of the victims. This part of the movie was about five minutes long, which is hardly enough to portray 20 years of victimization.

The murders are still a sensitive issue to many people whose families were either killed, accused or convicted during these events. The official end to the reign of terror was 1926 when the law was changed and the last of the appeals were exhausted. However, some claim the body count continued. The story begins in 1872 when the Osage Indians, a branch of the once-dreaded Sioux Nation, were given by their white fathers 1,500,000 acres of land, just south of the Kansas state border. The land was to belong to the Osage Indians, in the wording of the treaty, "As long as the water runs and the grass grows."

The white fathers were not known for their fair treatment of the Indians and the land given to the Osage people was no exception. The tribe developed a diet consisting mainly of meat, because the land was so barren it supported few crops. The Osage tribe was to suffer the same starvation and poverty endured by other Indian people, but the white fathers' dirty trick was about to backfire.

In 1906, oil was discovered on Osage land. More oil was found over the next few years and in 1912 one of the biggest oil strikes in the country was struck on Osage land. Generations of poverty had suddenly come to an end.

The 2,229 members of the Osage tribe each received an equal share or "headright" of oil money every three months. The spending sprees in the Osage Hills began. The Indians used the money to improve their living conditions by providing their families every modern convenience. One of the first things most of the Osage people did was to buy cars. It didn't matter that few Osages had ever been in a car and even fewer knew how to drive. It was soon recognized that there were more Pierce Arrow automobiles in Osage County than anywhere else in America. If an automobile was involved in an accident or needed repair, some owners abandoned it and spent up to $8500 on a new one. The excess spending by the Osage people became comical. The fact was there were many people who knew nothing of managing their new wealth.

The abundance of money and the outrageous spending sprees caught the attention of every con-man, thief and grifter. Price gouging became the order of the day and because of their seemingly endless wealth, the Osage people didn't seem to mind. Few of the Osage people understood things like compounding interest rates or complicated investment schemes. By 1915, regulations were enacted in an attempt to protect the Osage fortunes. By 1921, the regulations were strengthened to the point that none of the Osage people received payment without a certificate of competency. Those deemed incompetent required a legal guardian who would receive the quarterly payments on their behalf. Most of the guardians were honest and did only what was best for their wards, though one can see the potential for abuse.

Of all the ways to cheat the Osage people of their money, the most diabolical method was to marry an Osage Indian, then have your spouse's family killed. If a family member died, their headright would be divided equally among the surviving family members. With your spouse's family dead, the married couple would receive all of the money. If your Osage spouse died, all of the money would go to the surviving non-Osage. As long as crimes and schemes remain low-key, they're usually hard to prove. It's when the perpetrators of such deeds become blatant they cannot be overlooked. One example of this would be the events concerning the death of George Bigheart. A prominent Osage County rancher and banker named William K.

Hale was in charge of Bigheart's headright. Hale and his nephew Ernest Burkhart put Bigheart on a train to Oklahoma City to be treated for his alcoholism. After he began to get sober he called W. W. Vaughan, his attorney who lived in Pawhuska, and asked him to come to Oklahoma City to protect him. Before the attorney could reach his client, Bigheart mysteriously died. Vaughan believed his client had been poisoned and that Hale had been mismanaging his estate. The attorney boarded the Midland Valley Railroad train for his return trip to Pawhuska. He had asked the porter to wake him when the train reached Pershing. When the porter returned, Vaughan was not in his room nor was he on the train when it reached Pawhuska. The following day, a railroad crew found the attorney's body along the tracks where he had been thrown from the train after being shot in the head. The citizens of Pawhuska petitioned state officials to investigate the mysterious murders of the two men, which prompted Governor Jack Walton to assign special investigator Herman Fox Davis to the case. Shortly afterwards, the investigator was found guilty of bribery and sentenced to prison. He was later pardoned by the same governor who gave him the assignment. Needless to say, the deaths of Bigheart and Vaughan went unsolved.

February 6, 1923, two hunters found the body of Henry Roan (also known as Henry Roanhorse) who had been reported missing by his wife a week earlier. Roan's killer had left him as he died; slumped behind the wheel of his Buick with two rounds from a .45 caliber revolver in his head. Here again was another murder victim with a financial connection to William Hale in that Roan had borrowed $1200 and as collateral, had named Hale as beneficiary of a $25,000 life insurance policy.

A friend of Roan's named Henry Bennet was aware of the many mysterious deaths and unsolved murders that had occurred in Roan's family. Allegedly, Bennet told Hale that he was going to Oklahoma City to inform the governor about the shenanigans in the Osage Hills. Whether or not that conversation occurred is unclear, but one sure fact is that Bennet was shot and killed just two blocks from the state capital. The murder was never solved. Before arriving in Oklahoma City, Bennet had connected the dots in the murders for his friend Hugh

Gibson. After Bennet's murder, Gibson traveled to Oklahoma City to complete his friend's mission. Gibson was found murdered in an Oklahoma City alley. It would seem that those responsible for the murders wanted it known by everyone what happens to those who seek justice. By this point in the killings, those responsible for the reign of terror were becoming so brazen that they no longer felt a need to remain low-key. Kenneth Rogers was shot and killed by an unknown assailant, while he was sitting by a window in his own home reading a book. Sometime around three o'clock in the morning of March 13, 1923, William and Rita Smith's eight-room home in Fairfax was destroyed by a violent explosion so powerful it shattered the windows of surrounding homes. Rita was killed instantly, as was the Smith's housekeeper, Nellie Brookshire, whose mangled body had been thrown some distance from the house by the blast. William Smith was found nearby, still alive and was rushed to a local hospital where he died without regaining consciousness. These were no longer just mysterious deaths or random shootings that occurred in isolated areas. Now entire families were no longer safe in their own homes. By now, there was no denying there was an organized reign of terror in the Osage Hills and that it was in full swing. The body count had become too high to ignore.

George Albery, a member of the Osage National Council, conducted his own independent investigation into the Osage murders. His report pointed to a "guardianship organization" whose members were abusing their authority. Local authorities were able to use information from Albery's report to solve a few of the murders, but the Osage people still lived in fear.

Since the murder of Henry Roan took place on federal land, it fell under the jurisdiction of this new group of officers called the Federal Bureau of Investigation. In 1925, when the F.B.I. entered the case, they were attorneys and accountants who could conduct investigations, but had no authority to make arrests or even carry firearms.

The F.B.I. agents infiltrated Osage County under the cover of cattle buyers, insurance salesmen and other commissions that would bring one to town on business. They began to uncover information concerning the events surrounding the murders of at least 12 Osage Indians.

The majority of the murders including that of Henry Roan were all in one formerly large family who, until about two years earlier, had left two surviving sisters, Rita Smith and Molly Burkhart, their combined headrights totaling $135,000 a year. With the death of Rita Smith in the explosion, Molly was left with all of her family's headrights. The investigators learned the names of many people who may have been connected with the murders, but three specific names kept being repeated: William Hale, John Ramsey and Hale's nephew Ernest Burkhart, Molly Burkhart's husband.

Luther Bishop of the Oklahoma State Crime Bureau, unlike the F.B.I. men, was authorized to make arrests and carry firearms, so he, with the help of Thomas B. White, Sr., a former Texas Ranger, was placed in charge of the investigation. On March 11, 1925, Bishop and White arranged for Blackie Thompson, a notorious bank robber who was serving a term for murder, to be released from the state prison in McAlester, Oklahoma. In return for his freedom, Thompson was to gather evidence in the Osage murder cases for investigators, then rat-out his friends. Thompson did not let down the investigators and provided Bishop and White enough evidence for U.S. Attorney Roy St. Louis to take before a federal grand jury in Guthrie, Oklahoma. Thompson's testimony in court also helped the prosecution's case, despite his participation in a bank robbery at Avery, Oklahoma, only a few days after his release. The ex-con explained to officials that he was forced to go along with the robbery because the gang found out he was an informant.

Ernest Burkhart and John Ramsey were arrested and taken in for questioning. Both men admitted their involvement in the murders and signed confessions. They accused William Hale as having organized and ordered the murders. On January 8, 1926, Hale surrendered to authorities in Pawhuska, Oklahoma to face charges in the murder of Henry Roan. Hale was a prosperous rancher and banker who outwardly had acted as a friend to the Osage people. He had condemned the lawlessness of the Osage Hills and had even offered a $100,000 reward for information leading to culprits behind the reign of terror.

The three defendants were charged with the murders of Mr. and Mrs. Smith and their housekeeper, the murder of Henry Roan and the February, 1922, murder of another of Molly Burkhart's sisters, Anna

Brown. Of all the Osage murders, these three cases were the only ones directly linked to the defendants.

Ramsey later recanted his confession, saying he was sick with influenza and had been deprived of food and rest until he signed the confession. Burkhart also attempted to recant his confession, claiming he was tortured with electricity until he signed the statement. Burkhart soon changed his mind, confessed to his role in the murders and became a witness for the prosecution. Burkhart wove a complex tale involving people who hired others to commit certain murders and conspire alibis. The only problem was that most of these conspirators had died the same type of mysterious deaths as had many of the Osage Indians. On June 14, 1926, Henry Grammer, who was with Hale in Fort Worth, Texas during the bombing of the Smith Home, was killed in a car wreck. There was evidence at the crash site to indicate the car had been tampered with before the accident. Additionally, there was some evidence suggesting Grammer may have been shot before the car crash, but this wasn't proven. Curly Johnson, who was said to have been an assassin, died after drinking poisoned whiskey. Ace Kirby, also named as an assassin, was killed soon after Grammer when he was shot to death during an armed robbery. The store owner had been tipped off about the upcoming hold up. When Kirby entered the store, the owner was waiting – with a shotgun.

Hale's first trial ended with an acquittal after the jury deadlocked six to six. He was re-tried, found guilty and sentenced to 99 years in prison. Ramsey also was found guilty and sentenced to 99 years in prison, as was Burkhart, who did not fight the charges. Hale had been dubbed the "King of the reign of terror in the Osage Hills." When Hale and Ramsey were sentenced on October 29, 1926, some thought it was the final chapter in the tale of the Osage reign of terror. What really ended the murders was a federal law passed in 1925 making it illegal for anyone with less than half Osage blood to inherit a headright. By this time in history, the government protection really wasn't needed, because after the initial oil boom, the average monthly income of a headright plummeted to about $50.

The reign of terror in the Osage Hills did not end because all of the bad guys had been brought to justice. The majority of the machine put in place to victimize the Osage people was still out there. On December 6, 1926, about five weeks after Hale and Ramsey were found guilty, Luther Bishop, the State Crime Bureau agent who had Thompson released from prison and brought the case to the U.S. Attorney, was found murdered in his own home at 1515 NW 27th Street, in Oklahoma City. According to investigators, Luther must have been upstairs asleep when he was surprised by an intruder. There was a violent struggle which ended in Luther's being shot numerous times in the arms, back and chest with his own guns.

Burkhart was sentenced to the state penitentiary in McAlester, Oklahoma and Hale and Ramsey were sent to the Federal penitentiary in Leavenworth, Kansas. Hale appealed his conviction, but by May 30, 1929, decided not to appeal any further and began serving his time. It was odd that a man like Hale, who had political friends in Kansas and who was rumored to have ties with organized crime in Kansas, was sent to the same state to serve his time. It was equally odd that in a state where he had connections he had dropped his attempted appeals. Whether or not these factors played a part, on July 31, 1937, Hale was paroled after serving barely 11 years of his sentence. Ramsey was paroled four months later. Meanwhile at the prison in McAlester, Burkhart, the state's star witness, was not released until October of 1949. For some reason, Hale visited Burkhart twice after his release from Leavenworth.

No one knows all of the secrets surrounding the Osage Hills. Some say Hale's ultimate goal was to have Molly Burkhart killed, then to have his nephew killed, thus claiming to be the soul heir to almost $500,000 worth of accumulated headrights. In total, I counted 24 murders, including both Indians and Whites.

The climate of fear never completely left the Osage people, though it lessened with the passing of time. It would require much time to heal the wounds inflicted during the Osage Hills' reign of terror.

Chapter 10

Whiskey, Death and Good Times at Keokuk Falls

Aldridge Mill and Gin on the far side of Keokuk Falls on the North Canadian River. *Photo credit: Archives & Manuscripts of the Oklahoma Historical Society.*

By a vote of 180,861 "For" and 112,258 "Against," prohibition became the law of the land in the newly-formed state of Oklahoma. Taking effect on November 16, 1907 at precisely high noon, it spelled the end of violent towns just outside Indian Territory that thrived from the sale of liquor and other assorted vices.

Indian Territory was "dry," meaning it was illegal to buy, sell or even possess alcoholic beverages. Across the border in Oklahoma Territory it was quite "wet." As a result, seedy "liquor towns" popped up along the borders of these dry territories and usually flourished – where questions weren't asked and where outlaws could hide out in plain sight. Of all such towns, none was more dangerous than the town of Keokuk Falls. This blood-soaked border town in the far end of the Pottawatomie County panhandle was about a mile away from both the Creek and Seminole Nations. The Indian Territory boundary line was never on the main street of town, as has been erroneously reported by some sources. Dangerous men like Bill Doolin, Zip Wyatt, the

Christian Brothers, the Casey Brothers, the Kelly Gang and other badmen of lesser notoriety found the "Falls" to be a veritable sanctuary from the law.

There was a toll-ferry boat on the North Canadian River half a mile south of town. It was built early in the nineteenth century and brought people and supplies to and from the Seminole Nation just on the other side of the river. Eventually, it was replaced by a floating toll bridge described as a log raft reaching both sides of the river bank where it was securely anchored. Despite its description, the bridge was capable of supporting heavy loads including "hay burner" and "two yoke, oxen-pulled commercial" freight wagons. After statehood, the trail that lead through Keokuk Falls and over the floating bridge became part of the old Ozark Trail which led settlers through the county. The fee for crossing the bridge was two cents, unless you ignored the crude sign which read "Two-dollar fine for going faster than a walk."

Keokuk Falls was one of many saloon towns along the Oklahoma/Indian Territory border and was established on September 22, 1891, after the second Oklahoma land run. It was a bit ironic that such a violent and dangerous town was named for a peaceful Chief of the Sac and Fox Indian tribe, Moses Keokuk (1816-1903). The town named for the chief became known as the home of the infamous "seven deadly saloons." There were two distilleries in the Keokuk Falls area responsible for keeping the 62 saloons in Pottawatomie County stocked with keg whiskey. Willie Irick, a Government gauger who was slightly crippled with one leg shorter than the other, had the important and envied job of testing liquor at both distilleries. The one located on the south edge of town made a habit of dumping its waste mash into a gully behind its building. Free range hogs consumed the mash and amused the townspeople by stampeding down Main Street in an intoxicated frenzy, pausing periodically to become romantic.

According to the old-timers, there were two kinds of whiskey–the "fighting" kind capable of arousing the darkest, most violent evil in a man's soul, and the "loving" kind, which evokes a feeling of peace and love for one's fellow man. Unfortunately, there is no record of anyone in the town of Keokuk Falls ever having consumed any of the latter drink. Gang fights, shoot-outs, knifings and a number of other things that could kill a man happened daily to a point where it was actually regarded as normal. A. Q. Hern was a stagecoach driver whose route included Keokuk Falls. As Hern would approach the town with his passengers, he would announce, "Stop 20 minutes and see a man killed."

D. N. Beaty, an Oklahoma homesteader and owner of a saloon in Choctaw City, opened the first saloon in Keokuk Falls in 1891. It was named the "Black Dog Saloon" and soon became a well-patronized business. Its success caught the attention of Dr. N. Stutsman, a man better known for gambling, gunslinging and illegal whiskey peddling than for upholding his Hippocratic Oath. The doctor became a regular at the "Dog" and on many occasions tried to get Beaty to sell him an interest in the saloon. When Beaty refused to sell for the last time, the doctor made threats to put him out of business. This conflict was to be the source of much violence in Keokuk Falls.

Dr. Stutsman opened the "Red Front Saloon," igniting a bitter feud with Beaty over control of the liquor business. The profits at stake were not only from legal liquor sales, but also from the highly successful bootlegging business responsible for whiskey sales across the border in the Creek and Seminole Nations. Both saloons had loyal supporters who considered the cause so great they shot it out to the death with opposing rivals. The saloon wars sparked gang fights and in some cases, day-long gun battles. Since there was no town marshal, the length of any particular battle was determined by how long it took to run out of ammo. During one lengthy battle, Beaty dispatched a rider to the county seat in Tecumseh about 28 miles away to summon the county's first elected lawman, Sheriff Jim Gill. When order was finally restored, there was one man dead, two men injured and three dead horses littering Main Street. Sheriff Gill returned to Tecumseh with a wagon loaded with 12 prisoners arrested for the disturbance.

With tempers flaring from the latest conflict, Dr. Stutsman confronted Al Cook, Beaty's chief bartender, on the street with an order to get out of town. Rather than face a shoot-out with a more skilled opponent, Cook heeded the doctor's advice for healthy living and packed. A few hours later, as Cook was making arrangements to leave town, he bumped into the doctor who was in the presence of a deputy sheriff. On the board sidewalk in front of J. H. Patterson's store, an argument commenced between Stutsman and the former bartender. As the words began to heat up, the unarmed doctor pulled the deputy's six-shooter from its holster and began to fire. Cook, who was armed, pulled his revolver and returned fire; both men shooting point-blank. When the smoke cleared, both men were only wounded, Stutsman coming out the worst with a round in his stomach.

Dr. Stutsman was charged in the shooting while Cook was cleared of any blame. It looked as if the vicious bootlegger was about to face justice. However, the doctor had a few cards up his sleeve. Sheriff Gill and his deputy had the responsibility of collecting the 29 witnesses against Dr. Stutsman from Keokuk Falls to the county seat in Tecumseh. The day before the trial, the lawmen arrived with two wagons to accommodate the group that was the bulk of the prosecution's case. On the way back that night, the party was ambushed near Econtuchka by five of Stutsman's henchmen, including a man named Brewer who was one of Sheriff Gill's own deputies. All that happened was a volley of gunfire at the lead wagon which sent the horses bolting and the witnesses scattering. Considering the advantage of the shooters and the fact that no one was killed or injured, it would seem the doctor may have only wanted to send a message. In Keokuk Falls that night was another shoot-out between the two saloon factions. The battle ended some time around dawn when both sides ran out of ammunition. Casualties included a Creek Indian named Whiskey Bill and an outlaw of little significance named "Three Fingered Jack" (a Jackie come lately, not the original outlaw of notoriety from the 1850s) was further maimed when a bullet tore his right ear from his head.

Needless to say, Dr. Stutsman's trial was postponed. With little to fear from the law and the liquor business flourishing, Dr. Stutsman was ready to expand. In 1895, he purchased the distillery about two miles north of town from N.A. "Jack" Owens. At this point, after several years of fighting and thousands of spent cartridges, Beaty had enough. He sold the Dog to the operator of a small Keokuk Falls hotel named Aaron Haning. This got Beaty off the hook with the reigning liquor kingpin, but Haning was now the obstacle. Dr. Stutsman was determined to control all the liquor that flowed in Keokuk Falls.

Haning's stint as a saloon owner came to an end on the night of July 1, 1897, when he was shot in the forehead after going to bed in a rear room. Apparently, the shooter returned after awhile to find Haning still alive. To hasten his departure, a rusty nail was shoved into the bullet wound, then extracted and left on the window ledge for the sheriff to find. A witness reported seeing a shadowy figure after hearing a gunshot, but could not make an identification. It didn't matter because it was a sure bet that if Stutsman wasn't the killer, he probably had the job done. Sheriff Billy Trousdale conducted an investigation the next few days, then arrested Dr. Stutsman for the murder. Several months later, at a trial in Oklahoma City, he was found guilty of murder. Stutsman's attorney was of such a high caliber as to overturn the court's decision on a technicality, ensuring a second trial. After the second trial, the jury returned with a "not guilty" verdict and the doctor was free to return to the Falls and resume his reign; but instead, he saw the writing on the wall. He had pushed his luck too long in Keokuk Falls. Dr. Stutsman sold out of the liquor business and left town.

Despite the notorious reputation of Keokuk Falls, most of the town's residents were God-fearing, honest pioneer settlers; remember, there had just been a land run. Although the Falls never had a church, it did have regular stores and businesses just like any other town. Someone had to sell the ammunition, guns, clothes, food and anything else people needed.

The town of Keokuk Falls was surrounded in natural beauty. On the north bank of the Canadian River, by the waterfall for which the town was named, was a famous picnic area. In the mid-1880s, this same place was one of Sam and Belle Starr's "stops" they had established every 25 miles or so throughout the territory to "exchange" stolen horses, making them harder to track. During the summer months, the Falls were visited by thousands of people who came there to swim, fish and camp out. According to some accounts, catfish as long as five feet in length were frequently pulled from the river. For some strange reason, in and around Keokuk Falls could be found many types of animal oddities. Although no date was given, one exciting day citizens tracked down and killed a snake measuring 30 feet long! It was believed to have escaped from a circus. As the story goes, the snake's skin was given to an unnamed museum.

In addition to giant catfish and intoxicated swine, there was an auctioneer and postmaster of Vista (in the southern part of the county), Rufe Howard, who prior to the turn of the century would ride into town on a saddled ostrich. As a gimmick to draw a crowd before an auction, Howard challenged any horse and rider to a 100 yard dash against his feathered mount. According to all accounts, the out-of-place bird always outran the bewildered horse.

The most unusual animal find in the Keokuk Falls area was discovered by Bud Johnson. The son of Judge William Perry Johnson found the skeleton of a dinosaur south of the river in Gar Creek. The fossil remains were reportedly given to a museum in Chicago.

In Keokuk Falls, Big Ed Thomlinson and Mike Rooney were well-known. They were co-owners of one of the seven deadly saloons and also owned one of the town's two distilleries (the aforementioned distillery enjoyed by the hogs). The reason for their unchallenged success in such a dangerous business was due in part to Thomlinson's reputation and physical size. He was six feet, four inches tall, weighed about 250 pounds, and had killed the town's first marshal in a shoot-out. Thomlinson had been seeing the daughter of Marshal Jim Sweatte, much to the lawman's displeasure. According to accounts, the marshal drew first but Thomlinson was quicker on the draw and came out the better. Thomlinson was acquitted by a court who ruled the shooting of Marshal Sweatte "self-defense." William T. Sweatte, Jim's brother, was later made town marshal.

Bass Reeves, Deputy U.S. Marshall.
Photo credit: Archives & Manuscripts Division of the Oklahoma Historical Society.

Because Keokuk Falls attracted outlaws, it also occasionally attracted lawmen. Bass Reeves was one of the first Black U.S. Deputy Marshals in Oklahoma Territory. In a land where racial inequality and the Ku Klux Klan thrived, Marshal Reeves wielded the same respect and authority as any of Judge Isaac Parker's lawmen. Reeves frequently rode through the Falls in pursuit of badmen. Often he would be in the company of Ike Rogers, another Black lawman, until Rogers was shot dead by Clarence Goldsby, brother of Oklahoma badman Cherokee Bill.

During one pursuit, Reeves suspected an outlaw gang was hiding out in an abandoned log cabin just over the border in the Creek Nation. In order to avoid suspicion, he dressed as a poor tenant farmer and drove an old wagon with a yoke of oxen to an area close to the hideout. He then intentionally got the wagon hung up on a tree stump. Reeves knew the outlaws wouldn't want strangers hanging around and eventually would lend a hand to get him on his way. Just as predicted, the men appeared and proceeded to free the wagon. With the men offguard, Reeves simply reached into the pockets of his overalls and came up with two .45 caliber revolvers. After disarming the six outlaws, Reeves marched his prisoners in front of his wagon all the way to the jail in Tecumseh, more than 30 miles away. The six defendants were later sent to the Guthrie jail where they were held until convicted in Federal Court and sentenced to prison.

The last man hanged by sentence of Judge Isaac Parker, a.k.a. the Hanging Judge, had committed a brutal murder near Keokuk Falls, just barely across the Creek Nation borderline. James C. Casharego, alias George Wilson, was hanged at Fort Smith, Arkansas on July 30, 1896, for the murder of his traveling companion. The body of Zachariah W. Thatch was found floating in the nearby North Canadian River with two fingers shot off and his head split open with an ax. U.S. Deputy Marshal Eddie Reed (son of Belle Starr) was called to investigate the case. He investigated the area where witnesses saw the men camped. The shrewd lawman could tell there was something wrong with the layout of the campsite when he saw two burned-out campfires. One was in the center of the campsite and one against a tree. Realizing the campfire against the tree must have been an attempt to hide evidence, the investigator scattered the burned remains until he hit soil. There he found the earth still stained with blood. Reed collected chunks of the stained soil which was later presented as evidence in the trial. When the marshal caught up with Casharego, not only did he find the ax still stained with blood, but he also found blood on the man's trousers.

Casharego was a known thief who already had served prison time in Tennessee; now he had graduated to murderer. In pronouncing the man's death sentence, Judge Parker stated for the record, "Even nature revolted against your crime; the earth opened and drank up the blood, held it in a fast embrace until the time it should appear against you; the water, too, threw up its dead and bore upon its placid bosom the foul evidence of your crime."

Keokuk Falls did have "seven deadly saloons" for awhile, but throughout the years the total fluctuated. Seven saloons were the most at any one time, although some erroneous reports had the total as high as 11. The liquor that flowed inspired so much violence that by 1904, four of the seven saloons were ordered to close. The wild times at Keokuk Falls were nearing an end. Big Ed Thomlinson became Keokuk Falls' major civic leader, but he still had a reputation as a dangerous man. In 1906, Thomlinson was arguing in front of Oliver Templeton's restaurant with a none too reputable gunman named Felix Grundy. The exact events of the next few minutes would be debated, but one thing was obvious; Grundy had drawn his new .32 caliber automatic pistol and shot Thomlinson three times. The big man, with a round through his heart, staggered a few steps, then fell mortally wounded. Templeton, brother-in-law to Thomlinson, emerged from his restaurant firing his gun at Grundy who ran across the street into the store of J.H. Patterson. This might just be a coincidence, but at the time Grundy was employed by Patterson as a debt collector for his store.

Grundy was arrested by Sheriff W. A. "Bill" Grace for Thomlinson's murder. The prosecutor, County Attorney S. P. Freling, did not have an open-and-shut case. Many claimed Thomlinson was unarmed when he was shot. It was argued if he had been armed, Thomlinson's ability to quick-draw his pistol and hit his mark would have made him the winner. On the other hand, there were witnesses who claimed Thomlinson's wife ran to her dying husband and hid his holstered revolver in her apron. Due to the conflicting testimony, Grundy was acquitted. Without the civic leadership of Big Ed Thomlinson, the business community suffered a severe loss. Even before statehood, about half of the town's businesses had moved onto greener pastures. Places like Prague, about eight miles northwest of the Falls, were fortunate enough to have the Fort Smith and Western Railroad routed through their towns.

The day before prohibition became law in the new state of Oklahoma, Keokuk Falls toasted goodbye to its old way of life in grand style. The whiskey flowed as long as legally possible; then the party was over.

Without the lure of whiskey even the non-liquor businesses suffered. Without its infamous bars and close proximity to the railroad, no one had much reason to visit the Falls. A few residents stayed around, probably for sentimental reasons. These old-timers entertained listeners with colorful tales from the Oklahoma Territory days about shoot-outs and gang fights involving Oklahoma's most dangerous outlaws. When lawmen came calling, the outlaws rode two blocks north past the old frame school house, then took the road east a quarter mile to find sanctuary in the Creek Nation Indian Territory. In 1915, the Keokuk Falls' post office closed. Even the most die-hard residents knew the party was over after the spring floods of 1923. The famous waterfalls for which the town was named were no more. The North Canadian River had changed direction, covering the falls with silt and turning the once picturesque vacation spot into a mud hole. The following summer, the last store in town closed.

The spirit of daring and excitement had run out of Keokuk Falls. It was reduced to a ghost town holding many ghosts. As the years passed, all that remained were dilapidated old buildings surrounded by dust or mud, depending on the weather. As late as 1940, a family still lived in one of the old store buildings in town, formerly used as a saloon. In 1950, the Keokuk schoolhouse was physically moved to the Centerview School and the two structures were merged. Where the town's main street used to lie, a four foot creek later flowed for a few years. All that remains is the old cemetery to which there are no roads.

It's sad that this infamous saloon town that was such a part of the rich history of Oklahoma Territory is now gone and for the most part, forgotten. Perhaps, this is why people enjoy learning about the outlaw days of Oklahoma, so that these rich and colorful tales do not go the way of the state's many ghost towns.

Chapter 11
Four Men Hangin'

A few old photos from Oklahoma's past were made into postcards. One is a surreal depiction of a lynch mob's work simply entitled "Four Men Hangin.'" A simple picture that illustrates a young state's frustration with lawlessness. The events that led to the executions were equally vicious and violent. They tell a dark tale from Oklahoma's past involving blood feuds, a notorious killer for hire, and a vigilante conspiracy to murder.

At dawn, on the morning of April 19, 1909, the town of Ada, Oklahoma was unusually quiet. Hours earlier, a grizzly event had occurred. The morning light illuminated their deed – the kind of thing good people do only under cover of darkness. Next to the courthouse stood an abandoned barn. Inside, four men with nooses around their necks dangled from the crossbeams. A local photographer waited until the sun was bright enough to snap a picture. This could have been just one of many lynchings from Oklahoma's past – lost in time. Instead, captured on celluloid, was the timeless image of Oklahoma's most infamous lynching.

It is important to understand that Ada was not a lawless frontier town. It was a booming community whose residents took pride in their fine schools and seven churches. However, Oklahoma was a new state that had yet to shed its territorial ways. The events of that April morning illustrate the notion that people of opposing values cannot occupy the same space for long. The good people of Ada felt they had to set a few things straight.

Feuds die hard in the land of the Red Man. What ended in that old barn had begun years earlier, when the Sooner State was a wide open territory. Just two years prior to the lynchings Ada was on Indian Land. The South Canadian River 10 miles north of town marked the borderline between Indian and Oklahoma Territories. Prohibition was law for the Indian side in contrast to the opposite river bank where the liquor industry, both legal and otherwise, had thrived since 1891. Along this side of the border the deadly liquor boomtown of Violet Springs was settled. Entrepreneurs often supplemented legal profits by "bootlegging" their wears across the river. These criminal elements had only the threat of violence or death to protect their livelihood. Rival bar owners shot it out from their busi-

L. to R.: Jim Miller, Joe Allen, Barry Burrell and Jesse West hang at Ada, OK April 19, 1909.
Photo credit: Archives & Manuscripts of the Oklahoma Historical Society.

ness locations until ammo ran short. To make matters worse, the town's location was perfect for badmen wanted by the law. They could cross the river into Indian Territory where only Judge Parker's U.S. Deputy Marshals had jurisdiction.

The "Springs" as it was known, became a "Who's Who" of ill-famed Oklahoma outlaws. In such a place a man could lose his life for many reasons. The popular Corner Saloon, about three miles south of town, was the scene of at least 50 murders. The bodies of countless unfortunate victims were thrown into the river or buried without dignity behind the building. This earned the Springs a new nickname, "City of the Dead." In this bitter environment, a feud began between ambitious men. One that raged for years until all involved were dead.

Joe Allen and Jesse West were brothers-in-law who owned a rough and tough saloon in competition with the Corner. Most entrepreneurs face rivals, however these were ruthless men who responded to competition with violence. One night the men fired their guns into the Corner, destroying the entire stock of liquor. Although the owner at that time was no stranger to violence, he decided it was time to find

> **COUNTY TREASURER'S OFFICE, POTTAWATOMIE CO.**
> No. 81 Tecumseh, O. T. 5/27 1896
> Received of West and Allen
> the sum of Two hundred and no/100 ———— Dollars,
> Collected as Liquor Licenses
> from
> $200.00
>   J. H. Martin
>   COUNTY TREASURER.
>   By Ed Hard Dept.

Liquor License issued to Allen and West.
Photo credit: Herman Kirkwood, OKOLHA President.

a new line of work. J.M. McCarty, who already owned a couple of bars along the strip, became the new proprietor, and the next target of the feud with Allen and West. However, McCarty had allies who were socially influential and deadly. His personal body guard was the infamous train robber and killer Frank Starr. The feud intensified when Starr killed Allen's son Frank in a shoot-out in Indian Territory. At the shooting with Starr were two men, former jailer Sherman Carter, and an outlaw gang leader named A. A. "Gus" Bobbit.

Allen and West had been at odds with Bobbit for years since his days as a deputy marshal. He also owned interest in the Corner which only intensified any hard feelings. Bobbit's testimony in favor of Starr no doubt helped prove to investigators that Frank Allen was killed in self-defense. Incredibly, none of this was the main reason for the feud. Both parties were in the cattle business and, in the waning days before statehood, held grazing rights to sections of land in the Chickasaw and Seminole Indian Nations across the river. With Bobbit to the north and Allen and West nearby to the east, it wasn't long until charges of cattle rustling flew back and forth. This sparked a range war prompting both sides to hire teams of gunmen to protect their investments.

The nearest community of any prominence was Ada, also across the river from the Springs. It was a growing site of commerce which included cattle. As the cattle business came to town, so did the feud, dividing residents. On at least two occasion, Bobbit, Allen and West, and a few of their hired guns came close to shooting it out in the streets.

After returning from a trip to Texas, Bobbit experienced a "conversion." He changed his outlaw ways earning him the support of "good citizens" – those with political influence, members of law enforcement, and people of good standing in the community. His popularity was due in part to his membership in the local Masonic Chapter. The Masons have always been popular in Oklahoma and its members have influenced events since before statehood. Bobbit had achieved the prominent rank of 32nd Degree Mason. Allen and West, however, were unmoved.

In the midst of all this conflict, Oklahoma became a state in 1907. Prohibition became the law of the land causing the liquor boomtowns to go bust. Ada on the other hand thrived after statehood, absorbing the populations of many smaller, surrounding settlements. This included the unsavory elements from the Springs, and from further north, the liquor towns of Sacred Heart and Keokuk Falls (see chapter ten). The good citizens of Ada soon noticed they had a bad part of town. The not-so-good citizens had gravitated to a one block area where pre-statehood throwbacks continued their lawless ways. Within this area were two hotels and two cafes. As long as the rowdy elements kept to themselves, local law officers turned a blind eye to an increasing lawlessness. This included four bootleg saloons sporting legitimate store fronts known as "blind pigs." Ada citizens, shocked by the violence and death associated with this block, referred to it as the "Bucket of Blood." In one of these blind pigs known as "Ollie's" Allen and West found themselves most comfortable.

Statehood didn't just change the liquor business. Grazing rights in the area were no longer assigned by the Indian tribes, but by county judges. Bobbit, with his many connections, was able to acquire land for his growing cattle business. Allen and West, however, known for their shady dealings in the past, were denied consideration for land, effectively ending their cattle business in Pontotoc County. That was it – Bobbit had won.

Allen and West moved their cattle business to Canadian, Texas, in an attempt to make people think they were shed of the whole state, but they still had roots at Ollie's. Before leaving the Bucket of Blood they had solicited a killer for hire who was sure to do the job.

* * *

Of all the killers to grace the American frontier, the deadliest was a Texan named Jim Miller. More than Jesse James, Billy the Kid or even an in-law of Miller's named John Wesley Hardin, credited with 40 deaths. By today's standards, Miller was a serial killer. Although an official body count is hard to confirm, most authorities accept his claim to have killed 51 men. At the age of eight, he is alleged to have gun-down his own grandparents. As he matured he killed for reasons both business and personal. Miller dabbled in the cattle business and for a while worked as a lawman, but the true source of his wealth was known far and wide. He was an assassin for hire, and business was good.

Evidence suggests that Miller was hired to murder Pat Garrett, the former lawman who ended the life of Billy the Kid. In his book, *Shotgun For Hire* (University of Oklahoma Press, 1970), author Glenn Shirley makes the case that Garrett was lured to a location then shot from ambush. A New Mexico rancher named Wayne Brazil, one of two men riding with Garrett, was tried for the killing.

Unlike most infamous killers of the time, Miller was not an outlaw. The few times he was actually charged with murder he had deep enough pockets to hire the best legal council. Despite his reputation, Miller like Bobbitt, was a respected member of his community who could count on the support of powerful friends to vouch for his character. He didn't drink, smoke or chew, and his attendance and support of the local church earned him the handle of "Deacon." He certainly looked the part, dressed impeccably in his black suit. He was

Jim Miller, who was lynched in Ada, Oklahoma, April 19, 1909.
Photo credit: Western History Collections, University of Oklahoma Libraries.

also known to wear a long black coat with a frock collar, even during the warmest months.

Miller was no stranger to Oklahoma. Three years earlier, he crossed the Red River when he was hired to kill an Indian U.S. Deputy Marshal named Ben Collins. Miller was arrested for the murder and released on bond, but never had to answer for the crime.

The no-accounts at Ollie's agreed, if you needed an assassin, Miller was the man for the job. Bucket of Blood regular Berry Burrell knew him personally. Ollie introduced Burrell to Allen and West thus lighting a fatal fuse. Burrell agreed to travel to Fort Worth, Texas, and pay Miller a visit.

* * *

Bobbit knew there were men who wanted him dead. He also knew how easy it was for a man to lose his life in the vicinity of Ada, Oklahoma. You could arm yourself, your friends and workers, but that did little good in an ambush. The Bucket of Blood had become as outlaw friendly as the old Springs. By 1908, the area boasted 36 murders, well on its way to rivaling the Corner's body count. Still, the citizens of Ada did little to correct the situation. As long as the fight was near-fair and each side had a chance, the local court rarely convicted any of the participants. This was mainly due to the efforts of a famous attorney from Paul's Valley named Moman Pruiett.

In his career Pruiett represented 342 accused murderers. Three hundred and four were acquitted and the remaining 38 received prison terms from a few years, to life. Pruiett didn't come cheap, but if you could afford him, your chances of acquittal were almost guaranteed. He often boasted that if he ever lost a client to the gallows, he would retire from practicing law. But the town's people had begun to talk; something had to be done to stop the lawlessness.

On the afternoon of February 27, 1909, Bobbit was returning from Ada to his home, seven miles southwest of town. His neighbor, Bob Ferguson, trailed slightly behind, both men driving wagons loaded with cottenseed meal. A smartly dressed man in a long black coat, heading in the opposite direction arose no suspicion as he rode his horse passed the men. The stranger exchanged pleasantries with Bobbit before disappearing on down the road. Soon after, the men turned and entered the northeast corner of a field through a wire gate. In the fading light of day, Ferguson looked back to see the stranger just riding over a hill to his right. When the men were within a half mile of home a shotgun roared twice from an elm tree along the roadside. The first round struck Bobbit in his arm and shoulder. As he stood slightly, the second blast tore into his left side, fatally wounding him. He exclaimed, "Oh God," as he toppled headfirst from the wagon. His team broke loose running wild, and Ferguson dove under his wagon for cover. Peering through the spokes of the wheels he identified the shooter as the same man who had passed them on the road.

After the killer left, Ferguson unhitched a horse from his wagon, retrieved Bobbit's team, then rode to the dying man's house for help. Mrs. Tennessee Bobbit had heard the shots and was waiting on the porch in fearful anticipation. Her worst fears confirmed, she rode to her husband's side as Ferguson rode on to telephone for a doctor. It took Bobbit about an hour to bleed to death. There in the moonlight, he dictated his last will and testament to his wife. He rested his head in her lap, keeping his coat buttoned over his wounds. He told her he didn't know who had shot him, but was sure he had been hired by someone from his past. With his dying breath he offered a $1000 reward for the arrest and conviction of his killer.

Word of Bobbit's murder outraged the citizens of Ada. The town was slow to react when men killed each other in the street. Here, however, was a man shot from ambush while peacefully riding home to his family. Early the following morning Police Chief George Culver, with a posse of 24 men rode to the crime scene in search of clues. Tracks left by the killer's horse marked a clear trail. For 24 miles they rode north by northeast until coming upon a pasture south of the town of Francis. At this point, the horse's shoes had been removed. The land's owner was a 24 year old rancher named John Williamson, who received an immediate social call from the posse. At first he denied knowing anything about the horse, until a sharp punch to the nose cleared his memory. With blood streaming from his face he admitted a man had rented his horse for $20, but claimed he didn't know who. Another man grabbed the rancher's arm and twisted it behind his back, "You'd better talk," he informed the young man. Williamson pleaded that if he talked, he would be killed. His arm was twisted harder with the assurance he'd be killed for sure if he didn't. The terrified man exclaimed, "I had nothing to do with it! I swear! I want to see the sheriff – I'll tell all I know!"

Williamson was taken to the jail in Ada. That evening, he dictated his statement to Sheriff Tom Smith and County Attorney Robert Wimbish. He confessed that the horse's rider had been his uncle from Fort Worth, Texas, Jim Miller. He also claimed to have known nothing about the murder until after the fact, when his uncle told him to remove the horse's shoes.

"I killed a man," Miller had told his nephew. "Don't you say anything about it, or you're likely to get killed." According to Williamson, Miller repeated the threat three or four times.

Also named in the confession was a 19-year-old boy from the nearby town of Ardmore named Oscar Peeler. According to Williamson, Peeler was seen with Miller a couple of times before Bobbit was killed. Sheriff Smith wired a telegram to Ardmore Chief of Police Buck Garrett alerting him to the suspects in his area. The boy, Peeler, was known to work on a farm seven miles west of town. Thinking it might be a hideout for the notorious killer, the chief assembled a posse of lawmen and rode out to investigate. By this time Miller had already returned to Fort Worth, but Peeler was found and immediately arrested.

The youth turned out to be a hardcase. He knew the rules of the game, keep your mouth shut. Locked up in the Ada jail he refused to talk. Not even the knowledge of Williamson's statements seemed to shake him. The youth played it tough, until he was informed that County Attorney Wimbish was charging him as an accomplice to Bobbit's murder. That was all it took to get the boy to spill his guts, and he knew the whole plot and all the players. Peeler brought down the whole house of cards connecting Miller to Burrell, Allen and West. Authorities now had all they needed to charge the four men with murder.

On March 12, Burrell was the first to be arrested while attending a stock show in Fort Worth. Miller was next, also arrested by Fort Worth lawmen at a farmhouse outside of town on March 30. Both men waived extradition to Ada. As well connected men of means, they had little to fear. They knew the town's reputation for failing to prosecute defendants. What they didn't know was that the prosecution had Williamson and Peeler as witnesses.

Wimbish was sure that if Allen and West were arrested they would hire some crafty attorney to fight extradition – but the prosecutor was pretty crafty, too. He sent a telegram to Jesse in Canadian, Texas that read, "You and Joe come to Ada at once. Need $10,000. Miller." On the evening of April 6, the two conspirators were arrested after arriving at the train station in Oklahoma City. Only moments before, they had met with their defense attorney, Moman Pruiett, who himself had just arrived on a train from Paul's Valley. The men were tight lipped as they were booked into the Oklahoma City jail. With all four suspects in custody and two witnesses ready to testify it looked like an easy conviction for the prosecution. However, the wealthy defendants didn't seem worried. Their newly hired attorney inspired confidence in an acquittal. Their confidence soon eroded upon learning they were to be transferred to the Ada jail to await trial. The men begged to stay put. "He's [Bobbit] a Mason," Allen pleaded. "The Masons will kill us...they'll shoot us through the windows of the train."

West added, "They will shoot us through the car windows or the jail windows – any way they can."

They knew they were guilty, and so did Bobbit's friends and neighbors. Pruiett arrogantly comforted his clients. "You and Jesse are clients of Moman Pruiett. Nobody in Ada will bother you. We'll have Ada eating out of our hands if it comes to trial."

The following morning Allen and West were transported to Ada under heavy guard. They were promised by the officers if they encountered any trouble their handcuffs would be removed and their weapons returned. Despite their fears, they arrived without incident. Now Ada authorities had all five suspects, including Peeler, in custody. Williamson had been released on a $2500 bond. Allen and West knew their chances of acquittal were good, but they were in Bobbit's town. The citizens were angry, and sometimes murder defendants don't make it to trial. Lynchings were not uncommon on the American Frontier, however Ada wasn't some wide-open cow town. Still, how much more could law abiding citizens take? Deep-down the good townspeople knew they were to blame for the lawlessness. They had not held authorities responsible for the Bucket of Blood. Nor did they have the guts to convict killers when brought to court. Whatever the reason, the town's mood was ugly. Somewhere things had gotten out of hand. Decent, law-abiding citizens can be pushed too far.

Miller, however chided the population, referring to them as "stupid clodhoppers," going as far to say no one had the guts to lynch him. He wanted the whole town to know he feared no man or law. To Miller, arrests and courtrooms were an occupational hazard. Part of the deal with Allen and West included money for legal expenses. It was time to sit back and let the attorneys do their job.

In the meantime, Miller lived in the Ada jail like royalty. He had rugs brought into his cell and enjoyed fresh shirts daily. He dined on porterhouse steaks catered from a local restaurant. The killer shared his perks with his fellow inmates, except Peeler, which sent a clear message. Peeler and Williamson were soon sent to the Pottawatomie County Jail in Tecumseh for safe keeping until the trial. It seems Miller was even able to intimidate the judge presiding over his case. Before his April 16 preliminary hearing the court issued an unusual edict.

Order of the Court

In the Justice Court in and for Ada Township, Pontotoc County, Oklahoma, before Hon. H.J. Brown, Justice of the Peace.

Now on this, the 15th day of April, A.D. 1909, the Court of its own motion doth order that no reporter for any newspaper be allowed in the court room during the trial of the above styled cause for the purpose of taking the testimony introduced in the trial of same. It is further ordered that none of the testimony taken in the above styled cause shall be published in any newspaper in Pontotoc County. And it is further the order of this Court that the stenographer employed by the state to take the testimony herein shall return to this Court the original transcript of said testimony, when the same has been by her transcribed, together with any and all copies of the same which she may make or cause to be made in transcribing the same for her original notes of same taken on the trial of this cause.

The Court further orders the officers of this Court, including the Sheriff, Bailiffs, Constables, Deputy Sheriffs, Deputy Constables and all appointees of the Sheriff or any Deputy in attendance of this Court to search any and all persons they may see fit or may deem necessary, before or after any such person or persons enter the court room, for any weapons of any descriptions whatever.

The four men were ordered held without bail until trial, but everyone knew that was just a formality. Wealthy defendants, a scared judge, and Moman Pruiett; it didn't look good for the prosecution. It looked like once again, Ada would live up to its reputation as the town that tolerated murder. It seemed that its citizens were powerless to reign in the unsavory elements running loose in their streets. However, the victim in this case wasn't some sod buster or saddle tramp, they had killed a 32nd Degree Mason in turn-of-the-century Oklahoma. They might as well have shot the governor. It was time for the people of Ada to set a few things straight.

Since the hearing, rumors of a lynching had been whispered. It seems likely that local authorities were aware of the seriousness of the situation. However, security at the jail wasn't an issue. On the Sunday evening of April 18th, the Sheriff was out of town on "important business." The *Daily Oklahoman* would later report there were four guards on duty at the jail that night. In fact, James McCarty and Joe Carter who were reported as overpowered by the mob while standing guard outside, had also left town. The only two lawmen on duty were Deputy Sheriff Bob Nester and Walter Goyne, the city jailer.

The true story of what happened that night in Ada may never be completely known. Some say it was members of Bobbit's old gang who planned the lynchings. What is known is that there was a town meeting that evening that lasted until 2:00 A.M. Shortly after it adjourned, someone cut the phone lines to the jail. Two men entered the town's power station and ordered employees to turn off all street lights. In the ensuing darkness, a mob of about 40 masked men marched to the jail house and forced open the door. The two men responsible for guarding the prisoners were sawing logs in the sleeping quarters. Suddenly, 15 men with guns burst into the room demanding the master key to the cells. Deputy Nester showed true grit by reaching for his own gun, but before he could move he was hit over the head with a revolver. Goyne cooperated with the mob and handed over his keys.

The mob had been fairly quiet, but now it was time to make some noise. When they reached the row of cells where the four men were being held, the mob leader called out their names and told them to get dressed. The first one taken from his cell was Miller. The guards, who were now bound with bailing wire and themselves under guard, heard members of the mob questioning Miller, trying to get him to confess.

According to the April 21, 1909, edition of the *Daily Oklahoman*, *"A special agent of the state has reported that the mob when it went to the jail, had no intention of hanging other than "Jim" Miller; that Miller had been removed from his cell and taken out into the presence of the mob and examined for over two hours, and that at the conclusion of the examination the mob returned to the jail and took the other three men out and marched to the barn, where all four were hanged.*

"Miller, it is stated [by the guards] made an open confession in which he admitted having been implicated in the killing of A. A. Bobbit, and that he also told of other killings in which he had been implicated. The mob had assured Miller that he would be given a chance for his life in court if he would tell the truth, but that the telling of the story of past killings had so wrought upon the minds of the mob that the leaders could not control them, and the result was that all four men were hanged."

Whatever the reason, the four men were taken from their cells to an abandoned livery stable next door. West offered a futile resistance, and was hit over the head with a revolver, fracturing his skull. The others seemed predisposed to their fate. They were bound with bailing wire as the mob prepared a makeshift gallows. Much has been made about how Miller showed no fear in the face of certain death, and that he told the mob "All right. You've got a job to do, why don't you do it."

At this point, Miller probably believed his own hype, that no one had the nerve to lynch Deacon Jim Miller. That it was all a hoax, staged by little people attempting to unnerve a real badman. His bravado earned him the privilege of being the first man to swing.

Convinced of the mob's sincerity, he requested to have his diamond ring sent to his wife, and that Goyne receive his diamond stickpin. The jailer had been kind to Miller, serving as his personal bellhop for five dollar tips. Next he asked to die wearing his hat and famous coat. The coat was denied, and it isn't clear whether his hat was jammed sideways on his head before or after death. What is known, is that a noose was placed around his neck, and he was hoisted into the air. The proper means of hanging is for the condemned to drop a short distance, breaking the neck, which results in a quick death. Instead, Miller "danced on air" as it was called, until he lost consciousness. The exact last words of the killer are in dispute, but it is agreed that at one point he said, "Just let the record show that I've killed 51 men."

This grisly scene was played out in front of the other condemned men, who joined Miller in quick succession. Next was Allen, then Burrell, saving the barely conscious West for last. With the job successfully completed, the mob dissipated into the early morning darkness as a light rain began to fall.

Newspapers throughout the state, then across the country reported the lynchings. Many of the articles were accompanied by the already popular photo. Governor Haskell was openly angry at Ada officials who apparently had allowed the incident to occur. He ordered an immediate investigation into the events of that April night, but to no avail. A special grand jury convened for two and a half days without returning a single indictment. None of the 28 witnesses called to give testimony could connect even one name to the masked mob. The jury's report was published in the April 30th edition of the *Daily Oklahoman*. It read in part:

In summoning witnesses to come before us, we have had to rely upon the information furnished us by the guards at the jail, one or two county officers and what little personal knowledge we had of persons who were in a position to have seen the people who were supposed to have done the lynching.

We have had practically no assistance from the main body of citizens of the county and no person other than the ones above named has offered us any suggestions as to who knew anything of the alleged violations of the law, or where we could obtain any knowledge. We find from our investigation that the parties who took the four men from the jail were masked and that their identity was unknown to the persons who were before us, and that there were from thirty to forty men in the crowd. We have not had before us sufficient evidence to indict any of them, nor even enough to establish their identity.

It was learned that Miller's famous black coat had steel plates sewn into its lining. It seems he feared being killed by his own preferred style of ambush. The day after Miller's death, a New Mexico court found Wayne Brazel not guilty of the murder of Pat Garrett on the grounds of self-defense.

Mystery still surrounds that April night. Researchers have interviewed Ada residents for years in hopes of learning more about the lynchings. Like most mysteries, the official record becomes clouded by legend and hearsay. Some old timers have claimed there were no less than seven men hanged that misty morning. One account claims three ranchers arrived in town with bail money for Miller just after the lynchings. These men were then also hanged, but only until unconscious, then cut down and run out of town. However other details of this account were dubious. There were ranchers staying at the local hotel who had brought bail for Miller. In the February, 1967, issue of *True West* Magazine an article was printed about Miller entitled "The Last Ride." According to the article, the ranchers were run out of town, but it made no reference to any additional lynchings. Newspaper accounts at the time referred only to the "four men residing at the undertaker's parlor."

For a long time the people of Ada had talked about setting things straight. When they finally got around to it, they did a first-rate job. The word was out – Ada was no longer outlaw friendly. Ollie and his ilk got the message and left town. It was time for the Bucket of Blood to become just another block. To the dismay of the lawless, times had changed. Law and order had finally come to Oklahoma.

Record of Funeral.

No. 35
Date 2/28 19 9
Name of the Deceased _R. A. Babbitt_
Charge to _J. Stanfield_
Order Given by _____
How Secured _____
Date of Funeral _____
Place of Death _Ada, Okla._
Funeral Services at _____
Time of Funeral Services _____
Clergyman _Smooty_
Certifying Physician _____
His Residence _Ada_
Number of Burial Certificates _____
Cause of Death _Murdered_
Date of Death _Feb. 27-09_
Occupation of the Deceased _Farmer & Stockman_
Single or Married _____ Religion _Christian_
Aged _46_ Years, ____ Months, ____ Days.
Body to be shipped to _____
Size and Style of Casket or Coffin _6/3_
State Draped Copper Lined
Manufactured by _____
Metallic Lining _____
Outside Box _____
Number of Handles: _____
Interment at _Rosedale_ Cemetery.
Lot or Grave No. _8-10_ Section No. _20_

Price of Casket or Coffin	$150.00
Metallic Lining	✓
Outside Box	
Grave Vault	
Burial Robe	20.00
Burial Slippers and Hose	2.00
Engraving Plate	
Embalming Body (with ___ Fluid)	35.00
Washing and Dressing	✓
Shaving	
Keeping Body on Ice	✓
Disinfecting Rooms	
Use of Catafalque and Drapery	
Folding Chairs	
Candelabrum	
Candles	
Gloves	✓
Crape	
Number of Carriages _1_ @ $	
Hearse	20.00
Wagon Deliveries _Hack_	3.00
Death Notices in _Newspapers_	
Flowers	
Outlay for Lot	
Opening Grave	
Lining Grave	✓
Shipping Charges, prepaid	
Removal Charges	
Cremation Charges	
Notary Work	2.00
Total Footing of Bill	$232.00
By Amount Paid in Advance	
Balance	
Entered into Ledger, page ___ or below.	

Mch	4	To Funeral Charges Total	$232.00	c/-
Mch	15	By Cash		$100.00
"	26			132.00

Record of Funeral.
Photo credit: Herman Kirkwood, OKOLHA President.

Record of Funeral.
Photo credit: Herman Kirkwood, OKOLHA President.

Record of Funeral.

No. 60
Date: Apr 19 1909
Name of the Deceased: B. B. Burwell
Charge to: W. A. Burwell
Order Given by: ____
How Secured: ____
Date of Funeral: ____
Place of Death: ____
Funeral Services at: ____
Time of Funeral Services: ____
Clergyman: ____
Certifying Physician: Kim
His Residence: ____
Number of Burial Certificate: ____
Cause of Death: Hang
Date of Death: ____
Occupation of the Deceased: ____
Single or Married: Married   Religion: ____
Aged: 40 Years, ___ Months, ___ Days.
Body to be shipped to: Weatherford
Size and Style of Casket or Coffin: 6/3 State Oak ____
Manufactured by: ____
Metallic Lining: ____
Outside Box: ____
Number of Handles: ____
Interment at: Weatherford ____ Cemetery.
Lot or Grave No. ____   Section No. ____

Price of Casket or Coffin	75	00
" Metallic Lining		
" Outside Box		
" Grave Vault		
" Burial Robe	10	00
" Burial Slippers and Hose		
Engraving Plate		
Embalming Body (with ESCO Fluid)	25	00
Washing and Dressing		
Shaving		
Keeping Body on Ice		
Disinfecting Rooms		
Use of Catafalque and Drapery		
" Folding Chairs		
" Candelabrum		
Candles		
Gloves		
Crape		
Number of Carriages @ $		
Hearse		
Wagon Deliveries		
Death Notices in ___ Newspapers		
Flowers		
Outlay for Lot		
Opening Grave		
Lining Grave		
Shipping Charges, prepaid		
Removal Charges		
Cremation Charges		
Total Footing of Bill	110	
By Amount Paid in Advance		
Balance		
Entered into Ledger, page ___ or below.		
By Cash		

Record of Funeral.
Photo credit: Herman Kirkwood, OKOLHA President.

Record of Funeral.
Photo credit: Herman Kirkwood, OKOLHA President.

Record of Funeral.

No. 62
Name of the Deceased: Jesse West
Date: Apr 19 1909
Charge to _____
Order Given by _____
How Secured _____
Date of Funeral _____
Place of Death _____
Funeral Services at _____
Time of Funeral Services _____
Clergyman _____
Certifying Physician _____
His Residence _____
Number of Burial Certificate _____
Cause of Death: Hung
Date of Death: 4-19-09
Occupation of the Deceased _____
Single or Married _____ Religion _____
Aged 47 Years, __ Months, __ Days.
Body to be shipped to: Shawnee
Size and Style of Casket or Coffin: 6/0 State St Grey Plush Couch
Manufactured by _____
Metallic Lining _____
Outside Box _____
Number of Handles _____
Interment at _____ Cemetery.
Lot or Grave No. _____ Section No. 6

Price of Casket or Coffin	$75.00
" Metallic Lining	
" Outside Box	
" Grave Vault	
" Burial Robe	20.00
" Burial Slippers and Hose	
Engraving Plate	
Embalming Body (with __ Fluid)	25.00
Washing and Dressing	
Shaving	5
Keeping Body	
Disinfecting Rooms	
Use of Catafalque and Drapery	
" Folding Chairs	
" Candelabrum	
Candles	
Gloves	
Crape	
Number of Carriages @ $	
Hearse	
Wagon Deliveries	
Death Notices in __ Newspapers	
Flowers	
Outlay for Lot	
Opening Grave	
Lining Grave	
Shipping Charges, prepaid	
Removal Charges	
Cremation Charges	
Total Footing of Bill	$125.00
By Amount Paid in Advance	
Balance	
Entered into Ledger, page __ or below.	
By Cash	

L. T. WALTERS PAID APR 22 1909 ADA, OKLA.

Record of Funeral.
Photo credit: Herman Kirkwood, OKOLHA President.

Notice the people along the back wall peering into the barn. To the left of the photo, a small boy can be seen enjoying an unobstructed view.
Photo credit: Archives and Manuscripts of the Oklahoma Historical Society.

Chapter 12
Dad's Story

Joe Farris, my father, was born in Dewar, Oklahoma in 1914. He was in the perfect place to witness men who still lived like they were in wide-open Indian Territory. Since becoming "civilized" after statehood, even the smallest rural towns expected law and order; the only problem was enforcing such a radically new idea.

When my dad was eight-years-old, he was on his way to the local movie theater when he witnessed a shoot-out between a former deputy sheriff and four members of the Ku Klux Klan. I've heard my dad recount the events before, during and after the shoot-out and found them all interesting. In March, 1997, I contacted Ruby Wesson, Director of the Henryetta Public Library, to ask for help in finding more information concerning the shoot-out. Mrs. Wesson contacted Lois M. Rodriquez, a local historian and the owner/publisher of the *Oklahoma Citizen Newspaper*. Mrs. Rodriquez was able to find local newspaper articles regarding the shoot-out and Mrs. Wesson mailed the information to my parents' house, to everyone's delight; especially my dad's. With special thanks to the two ladies who found the newspaper articles, I now can detail my father's tale.

Tom Bouggous was a man who stood out in a crowd. Besides being outspoken, he was a large, powerfully built Indian who had lived in the Henryetta District for several years. He had been the city marshal of the nearby town of Dewar, but was removed from office about a year before the shoot-out, after being charged with the unlawful sale of liquor. A few months before his death, he had been reinstated as a law enforcement officer by a special commission from Governor Robertson. The responsibilities assigned Bouggous were not well understood, but there were three other men in this part of the country who had such a special commission.

The Ku Klux Klan was quite popular in the young state of Oklahoma and was used to doing whatever it felt was righteous. The Klan was responsible for crime and violence, which was ironic, because many of their members were lawmen.

In September of 1922, a group of masked Klansmen raided a hotel in the nearby town of Beggs. The owner of the hotel was alleged to have beaten his wife and the Klan was going to teach him a lesson.

The masked men carried furniture out of the hotel. Before burning the man's livelihood to the ground, the Klansmen invited all of the town's citizens to come and watch.

Some people in the area openly opposed the Klan. They had organized into two groups calling themselves the "True Blues" and the "Tiger Eyes." Bouggous supported these organizations and was himself an open and vocal opponent of the Klan and its methods.

October 29, 1922, fell on a Sunday. That afternoon, Bouggous had attended an anti-Klan rally in Okmulgee and had boasted he led a group hostile to the Klan. Later that evening, he was watching a picture show at the movie theater in Spelter City. Despite his casual nature, Bouggous knew he was a marked man and carried two large revolvers.

Around 7:30 p.m., two touring cars (big sedans with running boards) loaded with men wearing blue masks pulled up in front of the theater. Four of the men got out and sent word for Bouggous to step out and see them. Bouggous confronted the four men, who then exchanged words. About this time, my dad was walking to the ticket booth to see the movie; he never made it inside, but he did see a show.

Apparently, the motive of the Klansmen was to abduct Bouggous, but they had no idea that two carloads of men wouldn't be enough. As the Klansmen attempted to seize Bouggous, a struggle ensued. At this point, Bouggous was struck on the head causing him to fall; but when he hit the ground, he drew his guns and started firing. The Klansmen were heavily armed and returned fire with rifles and shotguns. Bouggous had gotten to his feet when he fired the last of his rounds. Despite the Klansmen's possessing superior weapons and having the odds completely in their favor, Bouggous was hit only twice; but that was enough. Bouggous had scored more hits and never ran for the safety of the movie house which would have endangered others. He stood his ground and emptied his revolvers, then staggered a few steps and fell on his back, mortally wounded, right in front of my dad. A constable named Davis emerged from church and fired nine rounds at the fleeing cars from his Sunday go-to-meetin' automatic pistol. My grandfather quickly collected my dad and took him from the scene. As the cars sped away, one of the Klansmen fell from the

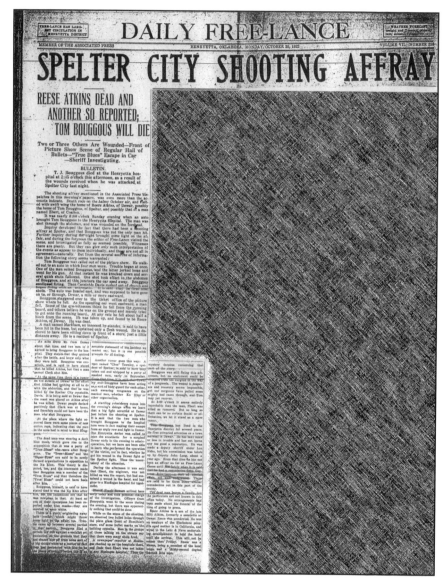

running board to the gravel street, dead, about a half block from the shooting. The dead Klansman was identified as Reece Atkins, a resident of Dewar. He was a respected man who belonged to the local Masonic Lodge and was a 32nd degree Scottish Rite man. Bouggous was taken to the hospital in Henryetta where he died the following afternoon at 2:45 p.m. Before his death, Bouggous said he had killed Atkins and that he had been shot by a man named Clark. It would have been hard to positively identify the masked men. It was suggested that the purpose of the blue masks, instead of the Klan's trademark white hoods, may have been to place blame on the aforementioned anti-Klan group, the True Blues. If that were the case, their strategy made no sense.

During the shoot-out, at least one bystander was hit. I say "at least one" because the first report I read mentioned the wounding of a man named Markham who was hit in the knee while sitting close to the fight. The second report did not mention Markham, but reported the wounding of a man named Spurlock. It could have been that only one man was wounded and the name incorrectly recorded. It is unknown whose shot did the wounding. It was soon learned that Bouggous also had wounded two of the Klansmen. Homer Pennequine, a deputy, and George Frew were identified as part of the raiding party when they sought treatment for their wounds. Both men were charged in the shooting, but released after a preliminary hearing. Since it was a small town, it turned out that one of the men charged, Homer Pennequine, was the husband of my dad's schoolteacher.

I don't think I would like to return to those days, but it's interesting to hear accounts from those who were there. It must have been an interesting time when law and order hung precariously from a thread; where only might made right and if you were connected, you could take part in the killing of a state appointed law officer and not be punished.

I hope this chapter will inspire other families to document exciting events from history witnessed firsthand by their elders. When one's history is forgotten, it is lost forever.

Chapter 13
Elmer McCurdy's Excellent Adventure

Many Oklahoma outlaws never saw a courtroom. Justice was often served at the barrel of a gun for badmen who resisted. More than a few Oklahoma badmen capitalized on their notorious reputations after lawmen ended their careers as outlaws. On release from prison, some former Oklahoma outlaws found work in show business. Henry Starr produced a movie depicting his gang's attempt to rob two banks at once in Stroud, Oklahoma and Emmett Dalton aided in a movie production of his brothers' gang's disastrous double bank robbery in Coffeyville, Kansas. An outlaw of lesser notoriety named Elmer McCurdy was probably the most successful in terms of show business, having appeared in a movie and on television. The fact that McCurdy had been dead about 60 years when he got his break is beside the point.

Elmer J. McCurdy was born in Maine around 1880. He was a bit of a drifter, having spent time in the army and in jail. His final years were spent as a hard-luck outlaw. Like many other Oklahoma outlaws, McCurdy emulated robbers who were successful decades earlier when law-enforcement was sporadic. McCurdy began his career as a train robber a few years after Oklahoma had become a state in 1907. Although there were still woods and hills where men on the run could hide, lawmen were better organized. By statehood, most badmen of any notoriety had been brought to justice. The Oklahoma badlands were becoming civilized.

By March of 1911, McCurdy hooked up with another outlaw of equal status named Walter Jared. The two men, with the help of some friends, robbed the Iron Mountain passenger train just south of Coffeyville, Kansas on March of 1911. The successful stick-up convinced the outlaws that they had found their niche and would make names for themselves as an infamous gang of train robbers. Brimming with false bravado, the gang made plans to rob a train a few miles southeast of Okesa, Oklahoma in Osage County.

At around one o'clock on a Wednesday morning, October 4, 1911, McCurdy and friends held up the Missouri, Kansas and Texas passenger train, number 29. For their trouble, they came away with $46, the conductor's watch and a couple of demijohns (large bottles with short, narrow necks and usually wrapped in wickerwork) of whiskey. If the gang had not been so anxious and waited just a short time after the M.K.& T., an express train would have come along carrying valuable merchandise and a considerable amount of money. The gang fled the robbery on foot into the Osage Hills. Two hours after the robbery, lawmen used bloodhounds to trail the outlaws into the Osage badlands, but the trail ran cold about a mile into the woods. Within a couple of days, Osage County Deputies Bob and Stringer Fenton and Dick Wallace picked up McCurdy's trail and followed it to an old barn on Charley Revard's place on the Big Caney River. The Saturday morning following Wednesday's robbery, the lawmen surrounded the barn. They could hear the outlaw's snores coming from the hayloft and decided to wait until he woke up and came downstairs. When McCurdy awoke around 7:00 a.m. to see lawmen waiting outside, he grabbed his rifle and opened fire. The deputies returned fire and the fight lasted about 30 minutes. After a while, the lawmen realized McCurdy had quit shooting. Cautiously, they ascended the steps to the hayloft to check on the outlaw. None of the lawmen was hit, but McCurdy wasn't so lucky. The deputies found him moments from death with a round in his chest.

McCurdy's body was taken to nearby Pawhuska, Oklahoma where he was identified as the outlaw in question, then left in the care of the local undertaker named Johnson. Sensing a chance to make some money, Johnson did something that was not too unusual at that time. He mummified the outlaw's body with an arsenic compound, then billed him as "The Bandit Who Wouldn't Give Up," and charged people a nickel to see him.

The undertaker exploited McCurdy to supplement his income until 1916 when a couple of men claimed that McCurdy was their long-lost brother. They convinced Johnson to give them the corpse so they could take him back home and give him a decent burial. Actually, the two men ran a carnival and had just secured a new attraction. McCurdy traveled with the carnival until 1925, when he was sold to a retired lawman named Louis Sonney who had a traveling exhibit called "The March of Crime." The owner's son Dan Sonney later explained to authorities his father was told the corpse was that of the outlaw Elmer J. McCurdy, but apparently didn't think it was real. Father and son covered the corpse in wax, then placed it alongside other wax dummies of villains.

Sometime around 1940, McCurdy and the "fake" wax outlaws were stored in a warehouse for almost three decades. Around 1968, Sonney sold the wax figures to a man named Spooney Sing (or Singh) who owned a wax

In his casket, overhead and side view: Elmer McCurdy, alias Frank Davidson, killed near Pawhuska in 1911.
Photo credit: Western History Collections, University of Oklahoma Libraries

museum on Hollywood Boulevard in Los Angles, California. McCurdy was billed as "The One-Thousand Year-Old Man" at a museum in the Nu-Park Amusement Park at Long Beach, California.

When the museum went out of business, McCurdy was transferred to Nu-Park's "Laugh in the Dark Fun House." The owner, who thought the figure was a five foot, three inch, 135 pound papier-mache prop, had him covered with florescent red and orange paint. McCurdy was hung by his neck from a noose and makeshift gallows, while illuminated by an ultraviolet light.

McCurdy would soon be eligible to join the Screen Actors' Guild. While in storage, Sonney had allowed his wax figures to be used as props. McCurdy appeared in a 1967 Dave Friedman epic called "She Freaks," but his big break was yet to come. On December 6, 1976, a scene from the popular television show *The Six-Million Dollar Man*, staring Lee Majors (or, for you cowboys, "Heath" from *The Big Valley*) was being filmed in the fun house. At one point, the director instructed a stage hand to move McCurdy to set up for a different shot. In doing so, the outlaw's arm fell off, revealing to the horrified stage hand human bones!

The Los Angeles County coroner's office collected the outlaw's remains. It was now up to the county's chief medical examiner Dr. Tom Naguchi to

Los Angeles County Medical Examiner's autopsy report of Elmer McCurdy.
Photo credit: Oklahoma Territorial Museum, Guthrie, Oklahoma.

determine the identity of the paint and wax-covered mummy and how he came to be. It was quickly determined the cause of death was a .32-20 caliber bullet jacket found in his torso. It became obvious to Dr. Naguchi that the corpse was many decades old. The use of copper-jacketed bullets began around 1905 and the practice of embalming cadavers with arsenic ended around 1920; at least he had narrowed down the time of death. Ticket stubs from the "March of Crime" show were found stuffed in the cadaver's mouth. The police began to question previous owners to determine the identity of the corpse. Dan Sonney was soon contacted and identified the mystery man as Elmer J. McCurdy, Oklahoma outlaw.

In April of 1977, Fred Olds, curator of the Oklahoma Territorial Museum in Guthrie, Oklahoma, Ralph McCalmont, Guthrie banker and historian, and Dr. Clyde Snow, Oklahoma City forensic anthropologist left for Los Angles to see if the body could be positively identified as Elmer McCurdy. Olds brought with him mug shots and a physical description of the outlaw. Dr. Snow, who was the chief of the Civil Aeromedical Institute's physiological anthropology research unit at the F. A. A. center in Oklahoma City, would look for scars and skin convulations to determine if the corpse was a match for McCurdy.

A technique called medical superimposition was used for the first time in Los Angeles County history to help identify the corpse. This is a process of superimposing an X-ray of the skull on a photo of the suspected dead man to see if they matched. It didn't take the experts long to determine they had the right (dead) man.

McCurdy's body was released and shipped to the custody of Dr. A. Jay Chapman, the state medical examiner in Oklahoma City. On Saturday, April 15, 1977, T. W. A. freight services flew the outlaw back to Oklahoma where his odyssey began. He arrived in a cardboard box and was unceremoniously loaded into a hearse to be transported to the state medical examiner. Dr. Naguchi refused to release the body to anyone but Dr. Chapman. The state medical examiner kept the body until it was to be laid to rest the following Friday morning.

On April 22, at 10:00 a.m., graveside services were held for Elmer McCurdy. He was laid to rest in the "boot hill" section of the Summit

Tombstone of Elmer McCurdy located at the Summit View Cemetery in Guthrie, Oklahoma.
Photo credit: Author

View Cemetery in Guthrie, Oklahoma, next to the grave of the "King of the Oklahoma Outlaws," Bill Doolin. Representatives from the Oklahoma Historical Society and the Indian Territorial Posse of the Westerners were present, as were others who paid their respects.

McCurdy's shipping and burial expenses were paid for by donations. The cemetery plot was provided free of charge by the City of

Guthrie. It was a way of paying respect to a long-lost son, who deserved the dignity and respect denied him for 66 years.

For those who know his story, it's hard to say the name Elmer McCurdy without cracking a smile. If McCurdy would have just surrendered to lawmen on that fateful Saturday morning back in 1911, he probably would have served only a few years in prison. Instead, he decided to take his chances with a rifle and the rest is history. A very bizarre history. But, before you laugh too hard, just make sure of your funeral arrangements.

Chapter 14
The End of the Trail

Entrance to Summit View Cemetery in Guthrie, Oklahoma.
Photo credit: Author

The last thing I had to do to finish this book was to take a drive to Summit View Cemetery in Guthrie. I needed some photos of tombstones that mark the resting places of outlaws mentioned in my book. Guthrie was originally the state capital and is awash in Oklahoma history. Almost anyone who lives in Guthrie can direct you to the town's famous cemetery complete with a "boot hill."

It was a pleasant summer day on June 8, 1999, as I drove my '71 Cutlass to Guthrie. I'd been to the town many times, but until that day had made no effort to visit the cemetery. With a little reassurance from the locals, I soon found the entrance to Summit View Cemetery. I drove past the rows of tombstones following the signs that lead to boot hill. As I brought my car to a stop, I could see a tall red and a tall grey tombstone which told me this was the place. I walked to the monuments and read the inscriptions. The red tombstone marked the resting place of the undisputed king of the Oklahoma outlaws, Bill Doolin.

The gray tombstone next to Doolin's marks the resting place of Elmer McCurdy. Although the inscription on his marker states he was laid to rest 66 years after his passing, it barely tells the tale of his post-death odyssey. It was a solemn moment, looking at the resting places of two men I had only read about. It reinforced the fact that these were real flesh and blood men, as opposed to fictional characters invented by a writer. I saw flowers and the remains of other gifts left by past visitors. I realized I had brought nothing to leave in honor of the men whose lives added so greatly to my book. Flowers didn't seem right for the outlaws; a bottle of whiskey probably would have been more appropriate. Instead, I removed a couple of rounds from my North American Arms .22 magnum "mini" revolver and placed one on each of the outlaw's tombstones. I stood for a moment enjoying a kindred spirit with my fellow Oklahomans, then took my pictures and left.

The pilgrimage to Summit View Cemetery's boot hill seemed to summarize the feelings I experienced while writing this book; a culmination of nostalgia and respect for a period in American

Tombstones of Bill Doolin and Elmer McCurdy located at the Summit View Cemetery in Guthrie, Oklahoma.
Photo credit: Author

history that will never come again. The times are always changing. Usually, for the better; at least we hope. By the time Oklahoma had become a state, most of the real outlaws were gone. Most were killed, some were in prison, the rest got smart and left for greener pastures. There were still a few hard cases around who didn't get the message, so lawmen would have to take the time to explain it to them. Before long, the outlaws on horseback would be replaced by gangsters with machine-guns, driving V-8 powered automobiles.

I have not been interested in the Oklahoma gangsters of the 1920s and '30s. It's hard to compare gangsters who cut down victims with fully-automatic weapons to the bravery of Ned Christie or the daring of Bill Doolin.

I think that's why so many people enjoy history. We know what happened. It's like reading a book you've read before and enjoyed. It's those memories of the past that bring a warm, cozy feeling to the present.

Index

Ada: 102, 105, 108, 109, 110, 111, 112, 113, 115, 116

Ames: 32

Ardmore: 110

Avery: 86

Beggs: 124

Black Mesa: 16, 17, 21, 22

Boise City: 23

Centerview: 99

Chowtaw City: 92

Daily Oklahoman: 39, 48, 113, 114, 115

Dewar: 124, 126

Dover: 32, 33, 34, 66, 67

Econtuchka: 93

Edmond: 30

Eldon: 48

El Reno: 32, 33, 34

Fairfax: 85

Francis: 109

Guthrie: 26, 33, 50, 51, 58, 63, 71, 72, 74, 86, 97, 134, 135, 136

Guthrie Daily Leader: 63

Hennessey: 33

Hennessey Clipper: 32

Henryetta: 124, 126

Ingalls: 50, 51, 52, 54, 56, 58, 67

Keokuk Falls: 76, 90, 91, 92, 93, 94, 95, 96, 97, 98, 99, 105

Lawson: 72

Locust Grove: 44

McAlester: 86, 88

No Man's Land: 17

Oaks: 43

Okesa: 130

Oklahoma City: 34, 64, 76, 77, 78, 84, 85, 88, 94, 111, 134

Oklahoma Citizen Newspaper: 124

Okmulgee: 125

Orlando: 26, 28, 30

Paul's Valley: 108, 111

Pawhuska: 84, 86, 131

Pawnee: 62, 63

Perry: 64

Pershing: 84

Prague: 98

Quay: 72

Red Rock: 60

Sacred Heart: 76, 105

Sinnett: 64

Skiatook: 60

Spelter City: 125

Stillwater: 27, 50, 51, 52, 56, 57

Stroud: 130

Tahlequah: 37, 39, 41, 42, 48, 79

Talala: 48

Tecumseh: 92, 93, 97, 112

Tulsa: 64

Vilas: 33

Vinita Leader: 48

Violet Springs: 76, 78, 102, 103, 105, 108

Vista: 95

Wharton: 26

Yukon: 77

"Oklahoma Outlaw Tales" References

(In order of appearance)

BADMEN FROM ROBBERS' ROOST

Patterson, Richard. *Historical Atlas of the Outlaw West* (Johnson Books, Boulder Colorado, 1985), p. 130.

Thompson, A.W. "Sole Reminders of Coe Gang Robbers and Murderers." Vertical files, Oklahoma Historical Society Library, not dated.

Killian, Bertha. "Robbers' Roost." Vertical files, Oklahoma Historical Society Library, April 12, 1937.

Wild West Magazine, "Badmen In No Man's Land," by Robert Barr Smith, pages 30-36, February, 1999.

OL' YANTIS BECOMES AN OUTLAW

Shirley, Glenn. *West of Hell's Fringe* (University of Oklahoma Press, Norman, Oklahoma, 1978), pages 121-126.

Wellman, Paul I. *A Dynasty of Western Outlaws* (University of Nebraska Press, Lincoln, Nebraska, 1986), pages 192-194.

The Edmond Oklahoma Sun, Friday, December 2, 1892, p. 1.

Patterson, Richard. *Historical Atlas of the Outlaw West* (Johnson Books, Boulder Colorado, 1985), p. 140.

BATTLE ON THE CIMARRON

Shirley, Glenn. *West of Hell's Fringe* (University of Oklahoma Press, Norman, Oklahoma, 1978), pages 272-282.

Patterson, Richard. *Historical Atlas of the Outlaw West* (Johnson Books, Boulder Colorado, 1985), p. 128.

NED'S FORT MOUNTAIN

Speer, Bonnie Stahlman. *The Killing of Ned Christie* (Reliance Press, Norman, Oklahoma, 1990), pages 29-39, 89, 123-129.

Patterson, Richard. *Historical Atlas of the Outlaw West* (Johnson Books, Boulder Colorado, 1985), pages 138-139.

The Oklahoma News, "Ned Christie, An Early Day Bandit," Sunday, March 14, 1937, section C, page 11.

Real West Magazine, "Ned Christie, Oklahoma's Mad Killer," November 1970, by George Hart, pages 18-20, 76.

Shooting Times Magazine, "An Oklahoma Tragedy: The Ned Christie Story," March 1999, by Sheriff Jim Wilson, pages 122, 120-121.

Strum's Oklahoma Magazine, "Ned Christie," Vol. 6, No. 5, July 1908, by W.G.D. Hinds, p. 78.

Harman, S.W. *Hell on the Border* (University of Nebraska Press, Lincoln, Nebraska, 1992), pages 552-555.

Nash, Jay Robert. *The Encyclopedia of Western Lawmen and Outlaws* (Paragon House, New York, New York, 1992), pages 74-75.

The Daily Oklahoman, "Cherokee Indian, Killed For a Murder He Didn't Commit, Exonerated After 30 Years," Sunday, June 9, 1918, pages 1-2.

Steele, Phillip. *The Last Cherokee Warriors* (Pelican Publishing Co., Gretna, Louisiana, 1987), pages 79-106.

HELL-FIRE AT INGALLS

Shirley, Glenn. *West of Hell's Fringe* (University of Oklahoma Press, Norman, Oklahoma, 1978), pages 149-166.

Wellman, Paul I. *A Dynasty of Western Outlaws* (University of Nebraska Press, Lincoln, Nebraska, 1986), pages 198-208.

Patterson, Richard. *Historical Atlas of the Outlaw West* (Johnson Books, Boulder Colorado, 1985), pages 136-137.

Oklahoma Gazette, "Outlaw Town," by Doug Bentin, October 28, 1993, pages 1, 3-5.

CATTLE ANNIE AND LITTLE BRITCHES

Nix, Evett Dumas. *Oklahombres* (University of Nebraska Press, Lincoln, Nebraska, 1993), pages 131-135.

Shirley, Glenn. *West of Hell's Fringe* (University of Oklahoma Press, Norman, Oklahoma, 1978), pages 305-308.

Carlile, Glenda. *Buckskin, Calico and Lace* (Southern Hills Publishing Company, Oklahoma City, Oklahoma, 1990), pages 45-49.

True West, "Cattle Annie Found," by Steve H. Bunch, April 1997, pages 10-13.

A BADMAN WHOSE WORD WAS GOOD

Shirley, Glenn. *West of Hell's Fringe* (University of Oklahoma Press, Norman, Oklahoma, 1978), pages 115-117, 321-329, 357-369.

Wellman, Paul I. *A Dynasty of Western Outlaws* (University of Nebraska Press, Lincoln, Nebraska, 1986), pages 228-235.

Nix, Evett Dumas. *Oklahombres* (University of Nebraska Press, Lincoln, Nebraska, 1993), pages 219-230.

Patterson, Richard. *Historical Atlas of the Outlaw West* (Johnson Books, Boulder Colorado, 1985), pages 134-135.

CHRISTIANS FROM HELL

Shirley, Glenn. *West of Hell's Fringe* (University of Oklahoma Press, Norman, Oklahoma, 1978), pages 283-301.

Patterson, Richard. *Historical Atlas of the Outlaw West* (Johnson Books, Boulder Colorado, 1985), pages 139-140, 142.

THE REIGN OF TERROR IN THE OSAGE HILLS

Franks, Kenny A. *The Osage Oil Boom* (Western Heritage Books, Inc., Oklahoma City, Oklahoma, 1989), pages 111-127.

Lamb, Arthur H. (The Sage of the Osage). *Tragedies of the Osage Hills* (Osage Printery, Pawhuska, Oklahoma, 1929), pages 150-181.

Wilson, Laura J. "Death Marches on the Osage Trail." Vertical files, Oklahoma Historical Society Library, 9/1/38.

WHISKEY, DEATH AND GOOD TIMES AT KEOKUK FALLS

Mooney, Charles W. *Localized History of Pottawatomie County, Oklahoma to 1907* (Thunderbird Industries, Midwest City, Oklahoma, 1971), pages 69-87.

Morris, John W. *Ghost Towns of Oklahoma* (University of Oklahoma Press, Norman, Oklahoma, 1977), pages 110-112.

FOUR MEN HANGIN'

Shirley, Glenn. *Shotgun For Hire* (University of Oklahoma Press, Norman, Oklahoma, 1970), pages 74-116.

Patterson, Richard. *Historical Atlas of the Outlaw West* (Johnson Books, Boulder, Colorado, 1985), page 127.

Clark, Charles N. *Lynchings in Oklahoma, A Story of Vigilantism 1830-1930* (CNC Enterprises, 2000), pages 63-86, (Provided courtesy of the Oklahoma Historical Society Library).

Morris, John W. *Ghost Towns of Oklahoma* (University of Oklahoma Press, Norman, Oklahoma, 1977), pages 202-203.

Berry, Howard K. *He Made it Safe to Murder, The Life of Moman Pruiett* (Oklahoma Heritage Association Publications, Oklahoma City, Oklahoma, 2001), pages 321-331.

True West Magazine, "The Last Ride," by William B. Secrest, Feb. 1967, Vol. 14, pages 6, 7, 8 ,9, 46, 47, 48, 50, 51, 52.

Ada Weekly Democrat, Friday, March 5, 1909, "Gus Bobbit is Foully Murdered," p. 1.

Ada Weekly Democrat, Friday, March 12, 1909, "Funeral of A. A. Bobbit," p. 1.

The Daily Ardmoreite, Monday, April 19, 1909.

The Daily Oklahoman, April 20, 1909, "Gruesome Light Greets Officers at Dawn After Three Hours of Bondage," p. 1.

The Daily Oklahoman, April 21, 1909, "Reward for Members of Mob," p. 1.

Ada Weekly Democrat, Friday, April, 23, 1909, Vol. 9/No. 38, pages 1, 10 (front and back pages).

The Daily Oklahoman, April 30, 1909, "Lynchers Not Indicted By Jury," p. 1.

DAD'S STORY

The Daily Free-Lance, Henryetta, Oklahoma, "Spelter City Shooting Affray," Monday, October 30, 1922, p.1.

The Henryetta Standard, "Two Men Die From Gun Fight Sunday," November 2, 1922, p. 1.

The Henryetta Standard, "Funeral of Reese Atkeson (Atkins)," November 9, 1922.

ELMER McCURDY'S EXCELLENT ADVENTURE

The Daily Oklahoman, "Bandit Slain in Desperate Fight with Officers," Sunday, October 8, 1911, page 1.

Saturday Oklahoman Times, "Outlaw Hits Comeback Trail," December 11, 1976, pages 1-2.

Oklahoma Journal, "Oklahoma Desperado Turns Up As Mummy," Saturday, December 11, 1976, pages 1-2.

The Daily Oklahoman, "Experts Hope To Find Out Is the Mummy Outlaw?" April 13, 1977.

The Daily Oklahoman, "Strange Odyssey Ending at Last," April 14, 1977, pages 1-2.

The Daily Oklahoman, "Outlaw's Mummy Back In State," Sunday, April 17, 1977, pages 1-2.

The Wall Street Journal, "A Corpse Is a Corpse, Of Course, Unless It's Elmer McCurdy," by Todd Mason, July 11, 1991, pages 1, 4.

Wild West Magazine, "Western Lore," by Robert Barr Smith, June 1999, pages 24-26, 75-76.

To receive a copy of *Oklahoma Outlaw Tales*,
send your name, address and $16.95, plus $2.50 shipping and handling to:

David A. Farris
P. O. Box 5991
Edmond, OK 73083-5991
(Please do not send cash)